TEA

MANUAL

for

HENLE

LATIN

SERIES

FIRST and SECOND YEARS

BY
SISTER MARY JEANNE, S.N.D.

LOYOLA PRESS.
Chicago

LOYOLAPRESS.
A JESUIT MINISTRY

www.loyolapress.com

© 1955
Copyright 1955
Loyola Press

ISBN 13: 978-0-8294-1204-8
ISBN 10: 0-8294-1204-2

Printed in the United States of America.
LSC/IRP 10/2021

TABLE OF CONTENTS

INTRODUCTION

The Henle Latin Series differs from the majority of the Latin series now in use both in its aims and in its methods. The Classical Investigation of the twenties, revealing as it did that many students drop the study of Latin after a single year and that few students attain to any real mastery of the language, led to a general acceptance of the principle that mastery should be subordinated to the presentation of material (especially in first year) interesting in itself and possessed of some utilitarian value. The author of the Henle Latin Series has chosen as his goals linguistic training and humanistic insight, which goals he believes should be reached through mastery of the language itself and through the study of classics selected and interpreted with a view to developing in the student certain attitudes, appreciations, and ideals.

He believes that a student, in order to obtain the greatest possible benefit from the study of Latin, should arrive at a certain mastery of Latin. If mastery was difficult in the past, the explanation is to be sought in the fact that the amount to be mastered was needlessly great and in the fact that the methods for arriving at mastery were poorly chosen. The Henle Latin Series provides for that amount of mastery which is essential. It concentrates all effort on the thorough mastery of the necessary forms, of the basic syntax, and of a practical working vocabulary. Forms, syntax, and vocabulary are not presented as things worth while in themselves, but as a foundation upon which can be built ability to read and translate Latin. The Henle Latin Series accepts whatever is good in modern methods of teaching without abandoning the traditional insistence on mastery of the fundamentals. It is therefore an integration of the old and the new.

This manual offers explanations and suggestions for teaching the first two books of the series, FIRST YEAR LATIN and SECOND YEAR LATIN, that will enable teachers to make the best use of the well-organized plan according to which these textbooks were developed. These explanations and suggestions are divided into three parts.

1

PART ONE: GENERAL PRINCIPLES OF METHOD

Teaching for Mastery

The modern subjects that have been added to the curriculum have produced a limitation of the time and effort available for the classical languages. There is no longer room for luxuries in the study of Latin. Thoroughness has become the most difficult of educational achievements, and it is possible only with concentration and economy of effort. The most fundamental of all the principles with which the teacher should be acquainted is the principle of teaching for mastery.

What does the concept of mastery imply? What is its nature, and how is it achieved? Mastery implies first of all *habitual* knowledge and *lasting* abilities. Good performance in a classroom recitation or a good showing in an examination for which there has been immediate preparation is not in itself proof of mastery. Habitual knowledge is knowledge which is always within the control of the mind and will and which can be recalled and used without previous reviewing. Hence the only adequate gauge of mastery lies in surprise tests and comprehensive examinations. Merely offering the matter day by day and being content with a good recitation on a limited area of prepared matter is *not* teaching for mastery. The knowledge carried over the summer, the knowledge that does not vanish within a few months after a test, is habitual knowledge. Most of us have an habitual knowledge of the multiplication tables. We have really mastered them. A student in third-year Latin who cannot, without preparation, recognize and analyze a purpose clause has no mastery of the purpose clause.

Besides habitual knowledge and lasting abilities, mastery implies *accuracy*. If a student cannot tell you whether the genitive plural of *rēx* ends in *-um* or in *-ium*, he does not have mastery. If he *thinks* that a certain clause is *some sort* of temporal clause, if he remembers only that a certain verb takes some case other than the accusative, if he selects the right mood for a construction but is not sure of the tense required—in all these cases his knowledge is not mastery, for it is not sufficiently accurate to enable him to do his work correctly.

Mastery also implies a high degree of *sureness*. If the student is guessing or if he thinks a form *might be* so-and-so, he has not arrived at mastery. The student must be able to *use* his knowledge and *assert* it with confidence.

Mastery implies, finally, *facility in use*. This facility admits of degrees, but if his performance is labored and slow, then certainly the student does not have mastery. If he declines a word with hesitance and many false starts, he has not attained mastery.

Mastery may therefore be defined as the *possession of a knowledge clearly understood, habitually and accurately retained, and easily reduced to practice.*

All the materials that form the basis of an academic course—facts, models, principles—should be reduced to this type of knowledge; it is the only knowledge that has real and ultimate educational value. In view of this fact it is clear that slipshod, scattered, and inaccurate knowledge has a positively deleterious effect on mind and character.

How is mastery gained? The initial step in teaching for mastery is that of the presentation of the matter to be learned. This presentation should involve activity on the part of the student and should as far as possible build—dynamically and intelligibly—on what the student already knows. For example, a student knows *servus* and other *-us* and *-um* words of the second declension. When *ager* is introduced in Lesson 16 it is presented by means of a development made by the student himself from his knowledge of *servus*. Merely assigning for memorization the full declension of *ager* is not enough. The student should be told that *ager* and other words like it have the same endings as *servus* except in the nominative, and he should then be required to complete the declension without referring to the GRAMMAR. Activity on the part of the student is a necessary part of the presentation of new matter. As far as possible he himself should work out the new developments. Memory unaided by thought is not likely to produce lasting knowledge.

The procedure followed consistently in the Henle Latin Series for presenting new material comprises three steps:

1. The student first sees a concrete example, which embodies the new point to be learned. This is in conformity with the normal process of thinking, for the mind understands the universal through apprehending the particular. A mere universal statement or rule means little unless supported by the concrete example. This is a vital point in teaching.

2. The student is then presented with a formula, a universal statement, and this he is expected to memorize. Accuracy and economy of teaching and studying are both impossible without a thoroughly mastered frame of reference, in this case a model paradigm or a generalized rule. Knowledge of the formula gives the student control over all instances similar to the example.

3. The first two steps are preliminary to the true learning. At this point the student can hardly be said to know the matter in hand. The knowledge has only a slight foothold, and practice alone will make it functional. As the third step the student is immediately required to go through the new matter. If it is a model, let him read it and point out the differences or similarities with models already learned; let him attempt to recite it. If it is a principle of syntax, he may run through a number of easy examples immediately. However clear the example and the explanation, the teacher will often find that students have not grasped the full meaning of the formal presentation. No teacher can make an abstract explanation so clear that correct use will follow as a matter of course. The immediate application of the formula in exercises is therefore imperative. It enables the teacher to see where additional explanation or correction of misunderstandings is necessary; it enables the student to see where his own understanding of the matter is inadequate or faulty. This practice is part of the presentation itself.

The presentation and the immediate active response of the student as described in these three points are only the beginning of mastery teaching. Written exercises and private study are now necessary to ensure successful participation in the classroom recitation of the following day. This recitation will then reveal any remaining inadequacies in the original presentation. It will usually be necessary to present a second time certain aspects of the matter, either to the class as a whole or to certain individuals.

This practice and supplementary explanation will have increased the student's understanding of the new matter to a large extent and will have prepared him to use it accurately. At this point the application of the mastery formula begins: testing, reteaching, and repetition over lengthening periods of time. By this means the teacher must see that the student converts his preliminary knowledge into habitual knowledge. The textbook provides exercises for private study and classwork, and the matter of one section is repeated in subsequent sections so that there is a constant review. In addition, systematic review exercises are found throughout the book. The teacher should go even beyond this in order to ensure adequate testing and repetition over lengthening periods of time, planning reviews and review tests to fit the needs of his particular class.

The following out of this formula requires the teacher to *plan*. He must keep himself informed of each item as it is taught, watching tests and homework assignments day by day, preparing daily programs involving continuous repetition that allows for everlengthening periods of maturation. The intervals at first should be very short; once presented, a point must be reviewed daily for some time in various ways; then the time should be systematically lengthened. Mastery requires a long period of time and the repetitions called for need not be elaborate or prolonged. A few minutes of classroom repetition are as effective as a long period, provided the matter is clearly brought to the attention of each student and is actively responded to by each.

The Latin Progress Tests, First Year and Second Year, may be used either for testing the mastery of pupils or as workbooks. They are objective, require little time, and are excellent for diagnosis and motivation.

Mastery teaching requires considerable planning and close attention to the progress and the difficulties of the class. In this course it is absolutely essential, the whole plan being cumulative. FIRST YEAR LATIN, and in fact all the books of the series, is so designed as to provide ample material for fast-moving groups and to lay the foundation for pupils unable to cover the entire book. The first six units are required matter for every class and must be covered by every teacher. But the exercises of SECOND YEAR LATIN review all of the essential vocabulary and grammar taught in Units Seven to Fourteen. A teacher who does not succeed in covering the final units need not be apprehensive concerning the ability of the class to read Caesar in second year if the pupils have thoroughly mastered the first six units.

It must be understood that points cannot be mastered all at once and that lessons cannot be prolonged with this intention in view. A period of rest or assimilation is essential. The formula indicates this. As soon as a preliminary mastery, a classroom-recitation mastery, is achieved, the teacher should go on to new matter, always of course keeping up the systematic review. The textbook is arranged so that this may be done with ease. It is well to take some new matter each day.

The exercises and lessons of the book are constructed and arranged precisely to allow for this type of mastery teaching. The subject matter of the course is divided into units, which cover certain large areas; for example, Unit One treats of nouns, Unit Three of verbs, and Unit Six of certain subjunctive forms, purpose clauses, and relative clauses. Each unit comprises a number of lessons and the lessons are in turn divided into numbered sections. Each section represents a short step forward, some new point to be learned and exercises to be used immediately after the presentation and for homework assignments. The exercises marked "essential" are those which are absolutely required for basic practice in the points being taught. They should never be omitted, and when time is limited should always be preferred to those not so marked. When assigned as written work they should be corrected by the teacher, and any important corrections should be explained.

A section is not intended to represent a day's lesson. Frequently it will be desirable to take two or more sections in a single class period. This arrangement in sections allows the teacher to determine exactly how much matter can and ought to be covered in the time available, and to stop at any point and still find exercises that adequately cover the matter just seen without presupposing anything not yet taught. In some cases the sections have a close logical relationship, and for these the vocabulary is adjusted to allow a faster progress, and the more elaborate exercises for written work are given at the end of the last section. Thus Sections 1, 2, and 3 of Lesson 17 have a single vocabulary, and translation exercises appear only in Section 3. All exercises are built up to repeat constantly the matter already seen. In addition special review exercises are provided to stress certain important or difficult points; for example, the gender of third-declension nouns.

Each section contains a certain amount of explanations, a basis for the initial presentation of the matter and supplementary to the corresponding formulae in the GRAMMAR. This does not mean that the teacher should say, "Read page 72 and memorize the declension of *magnus, a, um* as given in the GRAMMAR." He must give his own explanation in the classroom, and is free to give it in his own way, without, however, using different terminology or substituting his own rules for those in the GRAMMAR. To say "ablative of specification" when the author uses the term "ablative of respect" or to allow a different wording of rules than that given in the GRAMMAR is detrimental to the smooth progress of the course. Students will repeat these grammar rules and terms in second, third, and fourth years, perhaps under other teachers, and must not be confused. Individuality in the teacher is undoubtedly to be encouraged, but it should manifest itself in helpful explanations of what is in the textbook, not in the presentation of material at variance with what is in the textbook. Any other principle of action would result in confusion.

The Teaching of Vocabulary

Hardly less important to the success of this course than the method of teaching for mastery is the method of selecting and teaching the vocabulary.

It is in the realm of vocabulary that one of the fundamental points of difference in this series appears. The body of words chosen for this course is much smaller than that usually expected in Latin classes. The basic words have been chosen almost exclusively from the actual selections for reading that are to appear in second, third, and fourth years. All together, they provide a good general Latin vocabulary, free of words perhaps useful in elementary exercises but never encountered in Latin authors. There are almost no words used in FIRST YEAR LATIN that are not part of this basic vocabulary, and where such words do occur they appear as footnotes at the bottom of the page and are not meant to be learned. Throughout the four years the basic words are presented in exactly the same way, with the same spellings, parts, and so forth. From the moment a word is given for learning, it is expected to become a part of the habitual knowledge of the student. Thus every semester reteaches the vocabulary of the previous parts of the course, every examination presupposes the words that have been given in previous semesters. With this type of emphasis and repetition it is expected that knowledge will pass into habitual knowledge, acquaintance into mastery.

Emphasis and repetition are effective toward this end only because the presentation of the words follows a set plan. The words are given in the vocabularies fully equipped for action; that is, genitives, complete principal parts, constructions, and everything that is necessary for the intelligent and accurate use of the word is given. Furthermore, this "equipment" is made to dovetail with and complete the rules of the GRAMMAR. Thus, instead of a complicated rule for gender in the third declension, together with a long list of exceptions, the GRAMMAR gives a simple and easily remembered rule. Then in the vocabularies every noun following this rule is given without an indication of gender. Thus *lēx, lēgis* has no indication of its feminine gender, since it follows the simple SOX rule in the GRAMMAR. On the other hand, every exception to this rule is indicated; for example, *homō, hominis,* m. There need never be any doubt in the mind of the student about the application of the general rule if he has been taught the vocabularies carefully. The same dovetailing is made for the other rules; exceptions are duly marked in the vocabulary and are learned as part of the equipment of the word; unmarked words invariably follow the rule.

The rules of syntax are completed in the same way. Many rules, such as the one for noun *ut*-clauses or the accusative with the infinitive, cover a number of verbs, but of these verbs no common class can be formed. In the GRAMMAR, therefore, the rule is given so as to explain the nature and conditions of the construction; in the vocabularies every verb taking this construction is indicated by the simple notations *ut (nē)* or *acc. w. infin.* If this has been learned as part of the equipment of the verb, the student knows infallibly when to apply the rule of the GRAMMAR. The teacher should insist that the student learn, recite, and write the words precisely as they are set down. The vocabularies must be learned both from English to Latin and from Latin to English.

When a vocabulary is assigned for learning, especially in the first year, a prelection or preview should be given and the following points covered:

1. Make certain that the student understands all the abbreviations used.

2. Explain carefully any exceptional points; ask for the genders in cases where the rule is already known; for third-declension words ask for the genitive plurals as well and insist on an accurate knowledge of the general rules covering *-ium* words.

3. Be sure the class can pronounce the words. Read the words aloud and have the students repeat them after you. It is very hard for a person to memorize something he does not understand or cannot pronounce; the Latin student will approach vocabulary study at home with much less diffidence and reluctance if a start has already been made in class.

In the first and second years there should be *daily* review and drill on words, both in their stylized form as they appear in vocabularies and in phrases and sentences. Such review may be brief but should be repeated daily. The mastery formula—testing, reteaching, and repetition over lengthening periods of time—applies to vocabulary as well as to declensions, conjugations, and constructions. All tests should be cumulative with regard to vocabulary. The learning of vocabulary is obviously essential to progress in Latin; without it no systematic advance whatever can be made.

The Teaching of Declensions

The teaching of the declensions involves two main steps: (1) the presentation of models, which are to be memorized, and (2) abundant practice to reduce such models to easy recognition and use. The student can form or analyze most of the cases of Latin nouns that he will meet by means of one key rule and two supplementary rules. The key rule is: "The model to be followed and the stem are determined primarily from the genitive case." The two secondary rules are: "In the second declension the ending of the nominative (*-us* or *-um*) must be considered." "In the third declension the gender and the rules for genitive endings (*-um* or *-ium*) determine the model to be followed."

The following method of teaching the declensions has been found to be very successful:

1. Introduce the idea of declension. The beginner is often confused by the very notion of declension, since it appears to have no counterpart in English. The introduction of Unit One, pp. 3-5, gives the teacher some suggestions for presenting this topic by reviewing the declension of the personal pronoun in English. This introductory matter must be presented in some form by the teacher; it is not enough to have students merely read the explanation given in the textbook.

2. Present the model. Stress the stem, the endings, the meanings. At the same time present the rules for gender and the notes that accompany the declension.

3. Call for the declension of similar words once the model has been seen and the rules and notes are understood.

4. Require students to form individual cases as you name them and to identify and translate the individual cases.

5. Give exercises in which the students must analyze and translate such cases as they occur in phrases and sentences. This implies

a mastery of rules governing case usages. Such rules of syntax[1] are introduced gradually; for example, the dative of indirect object is introduced as soon as the second declension is learned, but other uses of the dative are explained much later.

6. Work for immediate recognition of case forms at sight and for quick recall for use in expression. This ability grows slowly with the students, but careful teaching in the beginning will help to give the student a growing sense of power and a corresponding eagerness to improve.

7. Review the declensions previously studied. After a new form has been introduced and mastered, present exercises in which the student is required to determine the model to be followed.

The command of forms and the understanding of the relationships expressed by these forms should always be kept in view. The following methods have been found helpful as supplementary to the formal training and drilling explained above:

1. Teach the student to reread Latin sentences after he has analyzed and translated them with a view to associating the meaning directly with the Latin words in the Latin order.

2. Teach him occasionally to read for comprehension in the Latin order, taking a sentence phrase by phrase.[2] The analytical method will serve as an accurate check on his comprehension and translation.

3. Use a bit of Latin in classroom situations: e.g., *ita, nōn, bene, quid? cūr?*

4. Have the student memorize and become familiar with good Latin sentences and phrases, such as the mottoes, selections from the Mass, and so forth. Emphasize that he should try to understand these directly, without a process of translation.

---

[1] The steps in teaching rules of syntax are those outlined above for mastery teaching: (1) formal presentation based on concrete examples; (2) immediate use in obvious and simple examples; (3) written work; and (4) continued formal review of rule and functional exercise according to the mastery formula.

[2] *Cf. On Reading and Translating Latin,* by Hugh P. O'Neill and William R. Hennes. Chicago: Loyola University Press, 1929.

PART TWO: FIRST YEAR LATIN

Unit One

The first unit teaches the regular declensions of the noun. Words like *sedile* and *animal,* known as *i*-stem neuters of the third declension, are not treated at all because of their relative unimportance. *Vir, puer,* and *ager* are postponed to a later unit. The main declensions thus appear in clear outlines.

The sections into which the lessons are divided are not intended to be taken up one to each class period. Many times two or more should be combined. Some are already combined in the textbook, one vocabulary being given occasionally to two or more points of new material.

Exercises are provided in abundance. Those marked essential, as shown in Part One, are those which must not be omitted, as they give basic practice in the points being taught. The others may be used orally in class, for written homework assignments, for review, or in any other manner or order the teacher may choose, or they may be omitted altogether when time is short. It is very effective to repeat orally exercises already done, or from these exercises to pick out certain sentences in which the class as a whole made mistakes and repeat them orally for several days. In such repetitions speed and accuracy should be demanded beyond that which was expected in the first writing. No teacher is expected to use all the exercises, especially in the latter parts, where more difficult exercises could be reserved for honor work; but frequently exercises which have been passed over may be returned to and used for rapid review or longer written assignments.

Before the actual work of Lesson 1 is taken up it will probably be necessary to make a certain introductory explanation of the alphabet and pronunciation. Gr. 1-5 provides the material. This may be treated simply or as a formal lesson with examples, drill, recitation, and oral exercises. If drill is planned, point to various vowels and diphthongs rapidly for a few minutes, calling for pronunciation. This can be done with a great deal of enjoyment, and even at this early stage the more alert students will begin to stand out.

It may be well to have the words of the Sign of the Cross or the Hail Mary printed on the blackboard or otherwise prepared so as to be legible to the whole class. This will serve for practice in pronunciation. Pronounce the words slowly and distinctly two or three times. Have the students repeat. Listen carefully for mispronunciations as you walk up and down the aisles.

Insist on two points for as long a time as may be necessary: (1) That a Latin word has as many syllables as it has vowels or diphthongs. (2) That syllables are never slurred in pronouncing Latin, but each one is pronounced carefully and distinctly.

Introduction, p. 3. As mentioned in Part One, it is necessary that the *idea* of inflection or declension be presented. The material in the textbook, pp. 3-5, is the basis for the teacher's explanation. It is not advisable to show the five Latin declensions at this time. The statement that all Latin nouns belong to one of these five groups is quite enough.

Since Unit One will cover the five declensions, it may be useful to have a chart ready which will show the five types of nominative and genitive forms, in some such manner as is shown in Gr. 25.

Some teachers may wish to show the plan of a declension also when the idea of inflection is being taught. This could either show the three cases only that the English declensions on pp. 4 and 5 show, or it could be complete. Do not require students to study this plan, especially the column showing uses, as the method of the textbook is to introduce the uses very gradually. If this outline is written on the blackboard it may be used when *terra* is being studied. Have a student insert the forms.

Case	Abbreviation	Form	Use	Meaning
nominative	nom.	....	subject	....
genitive (possessive)	gen.	....	possession	of or 's
dative	dat.	....	indirect object	....
accusative (objective)	acc.	....	direct object	....
ablative	abl.	....	adverbial phrases	....

Lesson 1, Section 1, p. 6. The general plan of presenting the declensions is to assign the paradigm to be learned completely and then to present certain rules and points of syntax to be studied simultaneously in order to allow use of the various forms. A slogan that may well be offered for the whole year's work is, "To learn Latin, learn endings." Gr. 31 shows the declension of *terra*. The endings should be drilled separately a few times.

Stress the importance of the genitive as the sign of the declension. The boxed rule on p. 6 should be memorized. All such rules are important and recapitulate some important point introduced in the section. The stem of a word gives some idea of the meaning of the word, but the exact meaning is indicated by the endings, as learned in Gr. 31. Do not hurry over the explanations necessary in this initial lesson. Detailed work here will help to lay a foundation for all the declensions and the conjugations also. Use the words of the vocabulary to point out genitive endings and stems.

Explain the rules for quantity and accent, Gr. 9-13. The rules given there should be memorized. Allow students to pronounce the words of the vocabulary without help as their first application of these rules. After this has been done have them try to decline the words of the vocabulary. Certain words occur only rarely in the plural, such as *Maria* and *glōria,* and need be learned only in the singular. (We could speak of "the two Marys." St. Paul speaks of *posteriōrēs glōriae.*)

Point out the difference between the nominative and ablative singular forms and add a warning that macrons are often a help in pronouncing and identifying Latin forms and should therefore always be heeded. In drills of any kind constantly connect meaning with form, especially when working on individual forms. Drills should be intensive and lively, but not continued over long periods of time. A great deal of variety is necessary to maintain attention and interest. The repetition of the first declension should be continued almost daily for some time. Various types of class procedure and drills will be found at the end of this unit of the manual.

The teacher should help students develop timesaving methods of mastering their vocabulary. In his own words, with whatever modifications seem desirable because of local conditions, he may speak to the students as follows:

"You will find that almost half your work is done if you know your vocabulary perfectly. Knowing your vocabulary makes other things easy.

"If you had to learn two hundred words before tomorrow morning to save yourself from being shot or hanged, you would learn them without any difficulty. Children much younger than you are have learned long vocabularies in a short time. Why not do what others have done and what we can easily do, and thus make all our work pleasant instead of hard and painful? Here are some simple rules that will help you. I am supposing that you will study your vocabulary from the printed book. There is another and perhaps better method which I will explain later.

"First, you have to want to learn those words. You have to pitch in and work. You must not just sit there and look at the words without doing anything.

"Second, say the Latin word to yourself, clearly and distinctly, and then say the English meaning clearly and distinctly. Use your lips if it helps you.

"Third, after you have said the words once or twice, close your eyes and see if you can say the Latin word and its meaning. If you know the first word, study the second word in the same way; then close your eyes and say both the Latin words with their meanings. Do this until you have learned all the words.

"Fourth, if the vocabulary is so long that you cannot remember all the words in the order in which they come, first cover the Latin words in the book with your hand or a piece of paper, and see whether you remember the English meanings. Then cover the English meanings and try to give the Latin words.

"I said that there is another and perhaps better method. This consists in buying some 3" x 5" cards at a stationery store. Write the Latin word on one side of the card and the English meaning on the other side. Use your cards every day. Look at the Latin word and see whether you know the English meaning before you look on the other side of the card; then take the same cards and see whether you can say the Latin word when you look at the English meanings. Put in one pile the cards that did not cause you any trouble and in another pile the cards with the words you did not know so well. Then repeat the words you did not know.

"There are two other suggestions that might help you. The first is to keep a record of how many words you can learn in a certain length of time; for example, in ten minutes. Another way of keeping a record would be to write down on a calendar the total number of words that you know perfectly on the date. Your record would then show you that on September twentieth you knew thirty words, on October first you knew sixty words, and so forth.

"The second suggestion is this, that you play a sort of game with some other student in the class, if you can get together somewhere after class. Using either the book or words written on cards, you ask him the meaning of a Latin word and then he asks you the meaning of another word. The winner is the one who knows the greatest number of words."

The important thing for the teacher to do is to convince students that they can learn a great deal far more easily than they imagine, and to get them to want to do the work. One means of accomplishing this that has been used consists in giving students ten or fifteen minutes to memorize the words in a mimeographed list that has been prepared. A test is given immediately and the scores tabulated on the blackboard. Emphasis is placed on how much can be accomplished in a short time, and questions are asked of individual students concerning their study habits and their success.

The vocabularies will always be followed by sets of related words, at first only related English words, but later Latin words also. The student is expected to deduce the connections himself. This effort will make the association more lasting.

Lesson 1, Section 2, p. 9. The explanation of gender on p. 9 is clear and concise and little need be added by the teacher. Although a knowledge of gender will not come into use until the adjective is studied, students should learn the rules of gender as assigned and from the beginning indicate the gender of new nouns as they appear. The habit of identifying gender can easily be established now and will make the study of third-declension nouns much easier. Make it very clear that the rule of natural gender (for example, nouns naming individual male persons are masculine) should always be applied first. Give some examples of natural gender in English, such as "king," "princess," and the like.

Lesson 1, Section 3, p. 9. The purpose of this section is to give sufficient knowledge of the verb for the construction of simple sentences. Formal study of person, tense, and so forth, will be explained in Unit Three. Call attention to the function of the endings as expressing the pronouns. It is possible that some students do not know that "he," "she," "it," and "they" are personal pronouns of the third person, and some may have difficulty in realizing that these pronouns can be expressed in the verb ending and need not be expressed by a separate word as in English. Do not, however, dwell on the personal endings in general. Only the third-person endings, singular and plural, are seen here, and the point to be taught here is *number* rather than *person*.

Diagraming is used to clarify the relationships of words in a sentence. Sometimes a student will see in a flash by means of a diagram what was cloudy because of his unfamiliarity with grammatical terminology. The method of diagraming used throughout the series is shown in GR. 1005-1017. The teacher will find that diagraming as a help in explaining syntax is very valuable. It is doubtful, however, whether students should be required to do much diagraming in the exercises. Some of the exercises in the first three lessons call for a little diagraming. Beyond that point the teacher must judge for himself the amount of diagraming he will require of the students.

Lesson 1, Section 3, Reading No. 1, p. 13. The readings are intended to develop an understanding of the Roman character and of Latin as a Christian language. Reading No. 1 is correlated with the pictures on p. 12. Call on those who are familiar with Latin phrases from having served at Mass or taken part in the dialogue Mass to recite some of the responses. Calling attention to the illustration showing the celebration of Mass on camp site and battleship will help to arouse interest.

Lesson 1, Section 4, p. 13. In schools where Latin is not restricted to the upper one fourth or one third of the students or where diagnostic tests are not administered before enrollment in the Latin class, teachers will find it necessary to test their students' knowledge of English syntax. Some students come to the Latin course with considerable knowledge of English grammar. Some will hardly know the meaning of "direct object." Methods of teaching differ so much throughout the country that no rule can be laid down on how much background grammar is necessary for the Latin student. If your students are already familiar with grammatical terms or after you have taught what is necessary of them, the following exercise may be used in teaching the accusative case:

1. The teacher or a student writes a sentence on the blackboard: — The sailor praises Mary.
2. The teacher asks: What part of speech is "Mary"? — Noun.
3. How is it used in the sentence? — As direct object.
4. In what case is it? — Objective.
5. What is the objective case called in Latin? — Accusative.
6. What is the accusative form in Latin for "Mary"? — *Mariam.*
7. Write the rule on the blackboard. — The direct object of a transitive verb is in the accusative case.
8. Write the sentence in Latin. — *Nauta Mariam laudat.*

The use of diagrams will also be of help in developing the accusative case, as is shown on p. 14. Drill on the accusative case can be done in the following way. Write a simple sentence on the blackboard; for example: The sailors praise .... *Nautae .... laudant.* Call for an object. Use all the words of the known vocabulary that can be used to complete this sentence. Run through a number of similar sentences. Require the student to recite the entire Latin sentence, not only the one word to be filled in. This also serves as a vocabulary review. The same plan can be used for other cases.

Some teachers may find it profitable to have the students identify each word in the sentence as soon as more than one case use is known, especially after the accusative case has been taught. This requires the students to concentrate on endings, the secret of learning Latin in the first year. Give three lines to each sentence, which will be parsed as follows:

Naut-ae	terr-am	laud-ant.
nom. pl., 1, m.	acc. sing., 1, f.	3rd pl.
subject	object	predicate

Two rules of position are given on pp. 14 and 15 (boxes). The simple rules of position given throughout the first year should be rigidly adhered to in student writing. Whenever variations are found in the readings explain that in Latin, as in English, unusual positions indicate emphasis; for example, "Him I despise!"

In connection with the accusative case and all other cases as they are learned, be sure that the students are mastering the idea that the case endings of the Latin words show relationships of words in sentences. This fact may seem obvious, but experience proves that it takes a long time for some students to grasp this important point.

During the course of the year, when the memory work seems to be getting burdensome, point out that young people learn and apply many complicated rules on the football field, baseball diamond, basketball and tennis courts, or that if some clever cheer or nonsense rhyme is going around, no time is lost memorizing it.

Lesson 1, Section 4, Talking Latin No. 1, p. 15. Students enjoy giving Latin greetings, and a deluge of questions may result from trying this in class. The usual comment made about this time is that those studying German, French, and Spanish are beginning to use phrases in their speech, while those studying Latin cannot do this. If you think it useful, add a few phrases or sentences to the *Salvē* they learn here. Beware of trying, however, to make the first-year Latin course a course in speaking Latin; much time can be wasted in the attempt. Learning to say a few things in Latin is merely a means of promoting interest and is incidental to the grammatical and analytical work.

Lesson 1, Section 5, p. 16. Stress the fact that the genitive case in Latin is used to express both the English possessive and many "of" phrases. After this case has been learned, the students are able to compose many original examples. Let them test one another with their own combinations.

Lesson 2, Section 1, p. 17. If the fundamental idea of inflection and cases has been sufficiently stressed, this lesson will present no difficulty. Drill students on the endings alone for a few moments before doing Exercise 10. Through reverence, since he is referring to the one true God and capitalizing the word, the author instructs the student to decline *Deus* only in the singular. At your own discretion you may explain that the word is used in the plural (as is done in SECOND YEAR LATIN) to refer to pagan gods. Even *Christus* can be used in the plural; for example, "There are not two Christs."

Lesson 2, Section 1, Exercises 11-12, pp. 18-19. Accustom students to translating phrases rather than individual words. The exercises are planned with this ideal in view. As can be seen in this section, exercises generally follow this plan: After the vocabulary the first exercise calls for *declension* of the new words and is followed by a *case identification* exercise. This in turn is followed by a phrase exercise; then come *Latin sentences* to be read and translated, and finally, when students have a complete grasp of the new matter, *English sentences* to be put into Latin.

Lesson 2, Section 2, p. 20. Considerable drill is required for mastery of the rule, "In all neuter nouns and adjectives the accusative is always like the nominative." To this rule may be added a helpful phrase, "and in the plural both cases always have the ending *a*." In calling for neuter nouns of the second declension you might require the following form: *bellum, bellī*, neuter, *a, a ; perīculum, perīculī*, neuter, *a, a.* By having to repeat the *a, a* for each noun of this class, students become alert to the distinction between masculine and neuter nouns of the second declension.

Lesson 2, Section 2, Exercise 18, p. 22. By no means omit this exercise, a review of principles. Students should be taught to regard any type of review lesson as very important. They may be told that, just as a merchant takes inventory at regular intervals to find out where he stands financially and to replenish his various kinds of stock, so they need to check their Latin stock, replenishing knowledge of vocabulary or syntax, relearning what may have been forgotten or only half-learned.

Lesson 2, Section 3, p. 22. In English the relationship of indirect object may be expressed by its own form, as in "Christ gave God glory," or by a prepositional phrase, as in "Christ gave glory to God." This will cause little difficulty if the point is made that the indirect object expresses the person or thing to whom something is said, told, given, or entrusted. Although only the verb forms *dedit* and *dedērunt* are used for some time with a direct and indirect object, it will prove helpful to repeat frequently: The verbs "say," "tell," "give," "entrust," and the like require a direct and an indirect object, because one always says, tells, gives, or entrusts something (the direct object) to someone (the indirect object). If this indirect object is not always expressed (as it usually is with these verbs), it is at least understood. Since the indirect object is generally a person, only *nauta* and *Marīa* from the first declension can be used here.

"To" should be given as the usual translation of the dative, although the paradigms in the GRAMMAR give both "to" and "for." The students may be instructed to use "for" only when the use of "to" results in awkward English.

The idea of the indirect object can be brought home only through many examples and much practice. Even so the student will not have a perfectly clear idea of it until he can compare it with those phrases which demand *ad*. Immediate practice should be given, and some help on the homework may be provided by running through Exercise 20 in class. In this preparatory work have the students merely point out the indirect objects.

Explain that the *ī* after *gladius* in the vocabulary on p. 23 is the sign of the genitive form. Note that in previous vocabularies the full genitive form has been printed. Vocabularies will no longer repeat the full form of the genitive except in special cases and in nouns of the third declension.

In order to establish firmly the habit of identifying the gender, from now on in the prelections on the vocabularies require the student to give the genitive form and the gender rule for all un-marked nouns.

Lesson 2, Section 4, p. 24. Call attention, first of all, to the boxed comment that some prepositions are followed by the ac-cusative case, some by the ablative, but none by the genitive or dative. The four prepositions given in the vocabulary provide opportunity for using the ablative forms for the first time and for a second use of accusative forms. There is no need to explain the ablative of accompaniment here, for *cum* and "with" as a transla-tion for this preposition is all that need be known here. The abla-tive of accompaniment will be specifically taught in Lesson 20 and distinguished from the ablative of means.

After commenting on the new vocabulary, p. 25, and before going through Exercise 22, form as many prepositional phrases as possible from the words already known; for example, *cum Mariā, cum nautā, cum nautīs, cum servō,* and so forth. Make certain that the abbreviations used in the vocabulary are understood.

Lesson 2, Section 5, p. 27. When teaching the predicate noun stress the *identity* of the subject and the predicate noun. Common sense will help students to see that the two words should agree in case.

The assignment requires the learning of certain forms of *sum.* By this time a teacher may expect questions on how to express first- and second-person pronouns, but it is sufficient to point out that these pronouns are shown in the translations of the six forms of *sum* on p. 28, and that each verb form *contains* an indication of the personal pronoun to be used in translating it. Students have little difficulty with the present tense of *sum.* There is no need to explain conjugation here; simply require students to learn the assigned forms.

Lesson 2, Section 5, Exercise 24, p. 28. Call attention to the agreement of *number* between noun and verb, noting especially the second-person forms such as those in sentences 8 and 16.

Lesson 2, Section 6, p. 31. *Quod* is introduced here in order to present the idea of a subordinate clause while remaining free from the confusing details of mood and tense. Also an opportunity is thereby offered for using complex sentences that are nevertheless easy. Only the use of *quod* with the indicative is to be presented here (GR. 572). There will be no difficulty if it is remembered that only sentences in which the reason is an objective fact rather than a subjunctive reason are to be expressed by *quod* with the indicative. The use of clauses of this type will make the idea of subordinate clauses already familiar when the more difficult types, such as purpose, relative, result, and other clauses are met.

Explain that "you" is expressed by the ending of *vidētis,* and "they" by that of *vīcērunt.*

Lesson 2, Section 6, Exercise 26, p. 31. This is the first exercise of connected paragraph material. Related map study can be made most interesting and informative. Have a student point out on the map the places named. A wall map could well be used. To use this exercise for a little practice in conversation, write *ubi,* "where," on the blackboard and then ask questions as follows: *Ubi est Gallia? Ubi est prōvincia?* The student at the blackboard points out Gaul, the province, and so forth.

Lesson 2, Section 6, Reading No. 2, p. 33. This may be an occasion for calling attention to the lists of related English words usually found after the lesson vocabularies. More than half of the words used in daily English speech are ultimately derived from Latin; for technical terms, of course, the percentage is much higher. The teacher may find *The Latin Key to Better English,* by Hart and Lejeune (New York: Dutton, 1942) a useful and interesting book. The study of derivation, however, should always be strictly limited and subordinated in the Latin class.

Note that at least one use has now been given for each case. By this time the student will have begun to acquire a practical mastery of the first two declensions in all the individual forms. Drills that may be used for practice in case forms will be found at the end of Unit One, pages 31-33, in this manual.

Lesson 3, Section 1, p. 35. The third declension requires careful treatment and explanation. The points that must be emphasized in the beginning are that the nominative has various endings; that the declension must be determined by the ending of the genitive singular *(-is)*; that once the stem is found from the genitive the noun can be assigned to one of three classes, the models for which are *lēx, pars,* and *flūmen.*

Stress the fact that the rules for *natural* gender are primary and should always be applied first. Show a number of English examples of natural gender, such as the following: postman, sailor, archbishop, queen, aviatrix, daughter. The ERROR, SOX, and LANCET rules for gender are crucial rules for the whole course. All nouns of the third declension not following natural gender or the three above-mentioned rules will have their gender marked throughout the vocabularies of the whole series. Hence it is sufficient to teach these rules only. If desired, GR. 52 may also be required, but the classes of words mentioned in this note are actually exceptions to the principal rules and will have their gender indicated whenever they appear. Each new vocabulary should occasion a review of the rules for gender. The material in this lesson is progressively planned so that with the proper drill students should master this declension with not much more difficulty than they did the first and the second.

Lesson 3, Section 2, p. 36. Do not allow students to get the false notion that one model is for masculine and the other for feminine nouns.

At least for a while require students to give the genitive plural of third-declension nouns whenever these nouns occur in vocabulary drill (see pages 93-98) or other exercises.

Lesson 3, Section 4, p. 38. Most students know this construction in English grammar and therefore have no difficulty here. In Exercises 36 and 37 you will find an appositive used in each of the cases with the exception of sentence 5, Exercise 36.

From this point on, brief quotations, proverbs, and mottoes are inserted for study and memory work. The mottoes (*sustineō ālās* [p. 135] for example) show one of the places in modern life where Latin still holds sway.

Lesson 3, Section 6, p. 44. Use Exercises 44 and 45 as a rapid drill. Repeat until a majority of the class can give immediate translations, especially from English to Latin.

Lesson 3, Section 7, p. 47. In the initial explanation of the vocabulary call attention to the note explaining *frātrum, patrum,* and *mātrum.* Since these words are exceptions (see Gr. 62), students should learn them as they appear, with the genitive plural written out.

Lesson 3, Section 7, Note on Reading Latin, p. 48. If the student is ever to read Latin as Latin, this type of reading must be encouraged from the beginning. He should be made to realize that Latin is a language, not a puzzle, and that he *can* eventually come to read it with a certain ease. Exercise 52 offers an encouraging beginning. These sentences can be read without difficulty if the vocabularies up to this point have been well learned. Later some of the better students may be given some simple reading matter and encouraged to develop a mastery of the language beyond that expected of the class in general.

Lesson 3, Section 8, p. 51. The declension of *flūmen* is presented as a problem to be worked out. The class should write out the declension according to the directions given in the text. This will bring out the precise points in which *flūmen* differs from nouns like *lēx* and *pars,* and the subsequent memorizing of the model will thus have some intellectual basis. It is well to remember that learning by rote, while apparently the simplest means of learning the basic forms in Latin, has two grave deficiencies. First, it does not as a rule give lasting knowledge. Second, the student who memorizes thus will throw needless burdens on himself. A clear understanding of the similarities and dissimilarities between words will not only assist the student's memory but will contribute in no small degree to his whole mental development. Admittedly, such teaching may not pay *immediate* dividends.

Call attention to the change of vowel in the genitive form in *flūmen, flūminis, iter, itineris,* and so forth.

Short formal drills on the first three declensions should be continued daily. Useful drills will be found at the end of Unit One in this manual.

Lesson 4, Section 1, p. 56. Review the basic principle that the stem is found from the genitive singular. The eight words of this vocabulary are the only nouns of the fourth declension to appear during the first two years, except *manus, ūs,* f., and *passus, ūs. Adventus, equitātus,* and *metus* are to be declined only in the singular; the plural of the other words need not be stressed, as these forms do not often appear. Neuter nouns of the fourth declension are so rare that they should be ignored.

Lesson 4, Section 2, p. 57. The proper use of *in* with the accusative and *in* with the ablative is sometimes mastered with difficulty by the high-school student and the points involved require constant practice. But if from the beginning *in* with the accusative is differentiated very clearly in idea from *in* with the ablative (that is, that the former always expresses motion or movement toward something), mastery will eventually result. It is not sufficient to make only a verbal distinction—*in* with the ablative meaning "in"; with the accusative meaning "into"—and this practice will only postpone the problem and perhaps make mastery impossible. Corrections on this point should be made carefully, with reference to the idea of motion or lack of motion. A periodic reteaching of *in* may be necessary, and mistakes and the consequent need for re-explanation should be expected by the teacher. It is useful to point out that *in* with the ablative usually refers to a place, while *in* with the accusative often refers to persons as well as to places.

Note that in the vocabulary *autem* is characterized as postpositive. Analyze the word "postpositive": *post* is from the Latin preposition meaning "after"; "positive," a variation of "position"; hence position or place after some other word in the sentence. You may add that "positive" is derived from the fourth principal part of the verb "place," *pōnō, pōnere, posuī, positus.* A simple reference here to principal parts, just incidentally, helps to prepare, although only remotely, for the study of the fundamental verb forms.

Lesson 4, Section 2, Exercise 67, p. 60. Observe the possibilities of this exercise: (1) It may be used as a translation exercise without reference to the questions below. (2) It may be used as a test of comprehension. Without calling for translation require answers to the questions in English or in Latin. (3) It may also be used to illustrate simple paragraph writing, the questions being used as a basis. The last suggestion is a bridge to Exercise 68. Train students from the beginning to see phrases that are to be translated as single units of thought, for example, "friends of Caesar," "into Gaul," "with the cavalry and (with) the soldiers," and so forth.

Lesson 4, Section 2, Exercise 69, p. 61. This is an excellent example of an entire paragraph in which the subject is expressed only once, in the introductory sentence, and contained in the verb ending, translated by an English pronoun, thereafter.

Lesson 5, p. 62. In explaining the vocabulary point out especially the difference in pronunciation between *aciēī* and the other genitives, and the two long vowels *-ēī*. Only a few words of this declension are in common use, and many of them are used almost exclusively in the singular. Drill *rēs* in all cases and uses; restrict drill on the other words in this vocabulary mainly to the singular. This vocabulary contains all the fifth-declension words to be met in the first and second years with the exception of *diēs, diēī,* m. (f.), to be introduced with the rules for time in Lesson 37.

Lesson 6, p. 64. The forms occurring here are not new. The point to make clear is simply the idea that some nouns have different meanings or different uses in the plural.

Call attention to the fact that, since *agunt* means "they give" when it has *grātiās* for an object, it may take an indirect object.

The picture of a Roman camp on p. 67 will help to make some of the vocabulary words more vivid. Boys and girls alike will find it interesting if it is presented with a little enthusiasm.

Review of Unit One, p. 70. This review contains a rather complete test on basic rules and forms of all the declensions. It may be repeated occasionally throughout the year so as to drive home the essential points. When Exercises 81 and 82 are assigned, the respective rules for gender should be asked.

As part of the review of Unit One or as soon as the fifth declension has been taught, a chart (see the next page) showing a complete "football" lineup can be used as an aid.

	FIRST	SECOND		THIRD			FOURTH	FIFTH
	F.	M.	N.	M.	F.	N.	M.	F.
Nominative	-a	-us	-um	....	....	....	-us	-es
Genitive	-ae	-ī	-ī	-is	-is	-is	-ūs	-ēī
Exceptions	nauta, ae, m.			collis, collis, m. mōns, montis, m.				diēs, diēī, m. (f.)

The two "ends" are feminine nouns, the "tackles" are masculine nouns plus the *-um* neuters, and the "center" is masculine, feminine, and neuter nouns.

A good plan for review of noun forms is to use work sheets of all the nouns learned so far or those that cause trouble, arranged in the following manner:

NOUN	NOM. SING.	GEN. SING.	GENDER	DECLENSION	MODEL WORD
1. agmen					
2. gladius					
3. glōria					
4. Rōmānus					

Formal Drills

The following devices for conducting drills have all been used with success. No teacher will wish to use all of them, nor would it be advisable to attempt to do so, for a certain amount of time is necessarily lost until students become thoroughly familiar with the routine of a drill procedure. Each teacher should use those forms of drill that prove effective for him.

1. Rapid recitation of paradigms for five or ten minutes, five minutes of silent study, recitation repeated.

2. Dictated practice tests in vocabulary, forms, phrases, and so forth. Read a number of items. The students write the answers. Now read the correct answers or let the class give them in concert. Ask for a show of hands on how many had five, ten, fifteen, or more mistakes. Do not record these grades. Allow five minutes' silent study. Dictate a second practice test. Give a quiz on the same material the next day or later. This exercise is useful for self-diagnosis on the part of the students, as it reveals the points where each needs to study.

3. Vocabulary test. Ten words is enough at one time. Students write declensions and gender for nouns, principal parts for verbs. Students who write less than 70 per cent correctly should be required to write out ten times each the words that were wrong.

4. Vocabulary test. Write ten words vertically on the blackboard. To the right of the word list place questions as suggested below. All these questions are to be asked about each word. Have each student answer one question.

king	1. Nominative singular?
leader	2. Genitive singular?
tribe	3. What declension?
shouting	4. How do you know?
father	5. What gender?
mother	6. What is the rule?
river	7. What is the stem?
law	8. How do you find the stem?
part	9. Genitive plural?
wound	10. How do you determine it?
	11. What is the model word?

5. Drill on forms. Have one student give the nominative and genitive singular (for example, *terra, terrae*). Have the class repeat these forms. Ask different students to give one form of the paradigm in correct order. Ask different students for different forms in jumbled order.

6. Drill on forms. Draw lines on the blackboard representing the cases. Point to a line and ask for a form.

SINGULAR		PLURAL	
Nominative	....	Nominative	....
Genitive	....	Genitive	....
Dative	....	Dative	....
Accusative	....	Accusative	....
Ablative	....	Ablative	....

7. Drill on forms. When declining adjectives, combine adjectives with nouns. Have one student decline the noun and another student decline the adjective.

8. Drill on noun forms and the agreement of nouns and adjectives. On the blackboard or on a large sheet of paper, in letters large enough to be read by everyone in the class, reproduce the table found on the next page.

dat. sing.	gen. sing.	abl. sing.	acc. pl.	acc. sing.	abl. sing.
dat. pl.	abl. sing.	acc. pl.	gen. pl.	abl. pl.	acc. sing.
abl. pl.	acc. pl.	gen. pl.	acc. sing.	abl. sing.	nom. pl.
acc. sing.	gen. pl.	acc. pl.	abl. pl.	dat. sing.	nom. pl.
gen. pl.	dat. pl.	abl. pl.	nom. pl.	dat. sing.	gen. sing.
acc. pl.	abl. pl.	nom. pl.	dat. sing.	dat. pl.	abl. sing.
gen. sing.	nom. pl.	dat. sing.	dat. pl.	gen. pl.	acc. pl.
abl. sing.	dat. sing.	gen. sing.	nom. pl.	acc. pl.	gen. pl.
gen. sing.	acc. sing.	dat. pl.	acc. sing.	gen. sing.	abl. pl.

On the blackboard write a numbered list of words. The list will vary from week to week or from day to day according to the point that has been reached in the textbook or the words on which the class has shown weaknesses and needs further drill. The following list is suggestive:

1. magnus homō	5. omnis spēs	9. longum agmen	13. via facilis
2. rēs gravis	6. amīcus fortis	10. lēx mala	14. sānctum nōmen
3. nōmen nōbile	7. longum iter	11. magna caedēs	15. magna urbs
4. breve iter	8. nauta malus	12. salūs commūnis	16. vulnus grave

Then, calling on the students by name or taking them in rotation, seat by seat, have each one give *magnus homō* in a certain case and number. You can say: "We will take *magnus homō* first and give the case and number called for. As I call on you, take the first line from left to right (or, the first column from top to bottom, or, the fifth column from bottom to top, and so forth)." One student then gives *magnus homō* in the dative singular, the next in the genitive singular, and so forth. The review can be turned into a game if a scorekeeper is appointed to keep a record of incorrect answers by aisles or by sides of the room. As a variation you can use a pointer to indicate the case and number, and call for the noun and its adjective by number. It is usually better, however, to follow the chart by lines or columns, as this ensures the same amount of repetition for each combination.

Game Drills

1. CHEERS. To drill declensions use cheers such as the "locomotive." First yell the endings forward, then backward; then go from nominative singular to nominative plural, and so forth. When the -um words occur, give a prolonged a for the nominative and accusative plural.

2. SONGS. Try setting words of the third declension to the melody of the "Song of the Volga Boatman."

3. RACES. Send students to the blackboard in teams of two each, to write paradigms or vocabulary.

4. STUDENT TEACHING. Now and then ask a student to conduct a review lesson or a drill. Students like to ask questions, especially in the form of a "consequence" game.

5. "AUSTRALIAN PURSUIT." Row works against row in a sort of relay. The first student in each row must answer correctly before the second student gets his chance. One slow student can upset the race for his row.

6. "SPELLDOWNS." These can easily take the form of football, basketball, or baseball games according to the season, as specifically described below in Numbers 7, 8, and 9. It is advisable to keep the same sides for some time. Make the prize exemption from a homework assignment. The losers will want to even the score, and keen attention is kept during the whole game. A teacher must be scrupulously fair in this game, as students will be quick to notice careless refereeing and scoring. Questions should be prepared in advance and should be of equal difficulty for both sides. In all "spelldown" games, as soon as a student misses a question he must sit down. In order to keep him occupied while the game goes on, have him write the answers. Any misbehavior in the line should be treated as equal to a miss—prompting, talking while

another is answering, slouching, and so forth. If this game is in baseball form, misconduct constitutes an "out" for the next inning or for the inning in progress should the offender's team be at bat.

7. FOOTBALL. Six correct answers in a row constitute a touchdown. If there is a miss, the other team gets the ball. The most interesting part of the game is the extra point. You ask the team captain to choose a man, a different man each time, to attempt the extra point. A certain amount of time is given. For example, as soon as the question is asked the teacher quietly says, "The center is over the ball, it's snapped, placed, and kicked." If the special man does not answer in that length of time, the kick is missed. It is usually a rather quick and bright student who has been picked by the captain, and the point is usually made. When it is missed the game becomes more interesting because of the one-point difference that prevails. If a team is answering a series for a touchdown when the class period comes to an end, the series in progress is not finished and does not count in the final score. The homework must be assigned in advance if exemption from an assignment is to be the prize.

8. BASEBALL. Teams are chosen. Every correct answer is a base hit. More than four correct answers before three misses constitute a run. Nine innings can be played during a regular class period if you move along rapidly. All hits are singles. This game is more interesting if you draw a diamond on the blackboard, advance the runners after each hit, and indicate the number of hits on a scoreboard. Thus, if the game ends with a tie in runs, the team with the greatest number of hits wins.

9. BASEBALL (a variation). Divide the class into two groups; choose a scorekeeper from each side and a bright pair of students for pitchers. A diagram of a diamond is drawn on the blackboard and a box set up for scoring. Each student may take up to four pitches (chances at a form, vocable, and so forth). One miss is an out, and thus the game moves rapidly. A base is gained for each right answer. The scorekeeper marks the runners' positions on the diagram and totals the runs and outs in the box. If a student asks for four pitches, answers three, and misses the last, he is out. He

must make all he asks for, or "they get him sliding into base." Three outs retire the side and the opposition takes over the pitching. If the pitchers proceed too slowly, have them draw up a list of questions ahead of time. If they still proceed too slowly, or ask questions that are too difficult, let the teacher pitch for both sides. The teacher is better able to adjust the pitches to the batter's weaknesses and will also judiciously repeat the missed items to give the students a chance to learn them.

Unit Two

Lesson 7, Section 1, p. 72. It is customary in many places for students to learn the adjective forms across rather than down; that is, they have been required to recite *magnus, magna, magnum, magnī, magnae, magnī,* and so forth. There are, however, certain advantages in requiring students to recite the paradigms of each gender separately. They already know the declension of nouns of the first and second declensions and have therefore the exact pattern of forms required. Besides, in checking errors a student can more quickly find the required form.

The declension of *magnus* is presented as a problem for the student, the working out of which will force him to make an immediate connection with the nouns he has already learned.

It will probably be necessary to discuss the use of adjectives in general, and the necessity of inflection. In this explanation the following points should be covered: (1) Unlike English adjectives, which remain unchanged whether they modify singular or plural nouns and whether these are in one case or another, Latin adjectives change their forms just as nouns do. (2) Up to this point gender has been distinguished in nouns but has not been needed for translating. Adjectives must also have gender, as gender is one of the points where agreement is necessary. Thus adjectives may be masculine, feminine, and neuter. (3) We shall not have to learn new endings. The endings for adjectives are the same as those for nouns, with a few exceptions. (4) There are two large groups of adjectives, those belonging to the first and second declensions and those belonging to the third declension. There are no adjectives of the fourth and fifth declensions. An adjective of the first and second declensions takes the endings of the first- and second-declension nouns; an adjective of the third declension has third-declension endings.

Lesson 7, Section 2, p. 73. The working out of the *magnus, a, um* paradigms and preliminary practice in reciting them will not take long. Go on as quickly as possible to this section on the agreement of adjectives. The important rule to be learned here is the boxed rule on p. 73. Now, the agreement must exist in *three* points: gender, number, and case. Students must be warned that this does not mean that the ending of a noun and the ending of the adjective modifying it will be identical. There is a tendency on the part of some students to make the adjectives agree with their nouns merely in the endings. The examples given in the text are deliberately chosen to prevent the formation of this notion, but the teacher must be alert to the danger.

For further exercise in agreement, have students change singular forms to plural and vice versa in Exercises 84 and 85. Adjectives are first used in sentences in Exercises 86 and 87. For extra emphasis on agreement have students indicate by arrows the noun to which each adjective belongs, as is done in Gr. 894.

The essential matter to be learned about the position of adjectives is summarized in the boxed rules on p. 74. The word "generally" makes provision for any exceptions that may occur for emphasis or other reasons.

Lesson 7, Section 3, p. 75. The use of arrows or another reminder of agreement is useful here. The examples on p. 76 or some of the sentences of Exercise 88 should be diagramed as shown for predicate nouns on p. 27.

In commenting on the vocabulary explain that "the rest of" is a one-word adjective in Latin, *reliquus,* and is not followed by the genitive case.

Lesson 7, Section 4, p. 77. In commenting on the vocabulary explain that *prō* may mean "before" or "for," but only in the sense of "in front of" and "on behalf of." This may be clearer if you express it thus: In front of or before a *place,* and on behalf of or for a *person*. Call attention also to the notation "pl., crops" and ask for other words they know that have difference meanings in the plural (*grātia* and *cōpia*). *Legiō*, although it follows the SOX rule, has its gender indicated because there is danger that students will consider it masculine because of its meaning.

An easy drill on adjectives may be conducted by using a single preposition such as *prō* with as many noun and adjective combinations as possible.

Lesson 8, Section 1, p. 82. The three points at which *gravis* deviates from the general pattern of third-declension endings should be carefully noted. Have students add *ī, ia, ium* when reciting words of this class to imprint on their mind these exceptions; for example, What is the word for "severe"? *Gravis, gravis, grave, ī, ia, ium.*

Explain the manner in which adjectives of this type appear in the vocabulary. *Gravis* is both the masculine and feminine nominative form; *e* stands for *grave*, the neuter form. The genitive is not given because the stem may be found by dropping the *is* of the nominative form.

Lesson 8, Section 2, p. 85. This is the first instance of adjectives governing a special case. The adjectives introduced here often cause trouble. The first step in trying to prevent this is to make clear that these words are, first of all, adjectives. As adjectives they must agree in gender, number, and case with the words they modify. Secondly, they sometimes govern nouns in English prepositional phrases.

To make this clear, take the sentence "They attack the neighboring town." "Town" is the object of "attack." *Fīnitimus* must be accusative neuter singular because "town," which it modifies, is accusative neuter singular.

Next take the sentence "They attack the town neighboring on the river." *Fīnitimus* agrees with *oppidum* as before, but the case of "on the river" depends on *fīnitimus*. This word takes the dative case; therefore, *flūminī*.

It is well to stress that, because *fīnitimus* is an adjective, it must modify and agree with a noun; it may also govern a second noun which will be put in the dative case. The proper case to be used depends upon which one of these special adjectives occurs in the Latin sentence, not on the preposition which is used in the English translation. The adjectives studied here, of course, are sometimes used without a modifying phrase. The words of this vocabulary must be learned as given, with the abbreviations indicating the cases to be used.

Lesson 8, Section 3, p. 87. In commenting on the vocabulary use sentence 1 in Exercise 101 to explain *et . . . et*. *Quid* is used here without any reference to its declension. It will be used only in such sentences as do not call for a change of form. The forms of the name *Jēsūs* must simply be memorized.

If the Sign of the Cross has not already been taught, teach it now and use it at the beginning of class.

Mastery Review Vocabulary No. 1, p. 91. This is a complete classified list of all the words learned thus far. It may be used in a number of ways: (1) A systematic review of this list day by day may be conducted on a cumulative plan, at the rate of a set number of additional words per day. The learning of words is perhaps the most important single item in the learning of a language. (2) Since the nouns are arranged according to declensions, these lists may be used as the basis for drill on case forms. (3) Definite pages or divisions may be assigned for each day of the week. (4) Assignments may be made on the basis of parts of speech; for example, nouns on Monday, adjectives on Tuesday, prepositions on Wednesday, conjunctions, adverbs, and other words on Thursday, and review on Friday.

Unit Three

Lesson 9, Introduction, p. 99. This introduction gives a grammatical explanation of verbs. Unless the students have had a good foundation in systematic English grammar this explanation is necessary. The boxed rules summarize important fundamentals often not clearly understood by all students.

Many a student who up to this time has done excellent work meets his Waterloo shortly after the study of the verb is begun.

The reason probably is (except in the case of students who are incapable of learning any difficult subject or who are unwilling to work) that the teacher proceeds too rapidly. The secret of good teaching here is to proceed by very short steps, giving multiple examples when necessary to illustrate each new point, and to emphasize the necessity of earnest study. For example, that verbs change their form to express different persons and also change their form to show number is a fundamental concept that may seem obvious, but is not so to all. Do not go on to a discussion of principal parts and the first conjugation until you are sure the material of the introduction is familiar.

Lesson 9, Section 1, p. 101. It is important in the study of verbs, as in the study of nouns, to recognize the *stem*. The four principal parts will indicate the stems upon which all the forms of the verb are built. It is sufficient in this section to cover the following points: (1) The principal parts of a verb give us the stems. (2) There are four main groups of verbs called conjugations. (3) The conjugation is determined by the present infinitive active, in which part the characteristic vowel is seen: in the first conjugation this vowel is *ā*.

Lesson 9, Section 2, p. 102. If necessary, expand the explanation of the endings as indicating person as follows: If *I* am doing something, the personal sign will be *-ō* or *-m*. If *you* (one person) are doing something, the personal sign will be *-s*. If *he, she,* or *it* is doing something, the personal sign will be *-t*, and so forth. Note, however, that the complete endings include the characteristic vowel of the conjugation as well as the personal signs.

The three English forms which correspond to the Latin present form should be kept clearly before the students. This will be done if the meanings are studied at the same time as the forms of the models, as suggested in the Assignment on p. 102, and if the three translations are frequently required in the exercises.

In commenting on the vocabulary, note that "get ready" is expressed by a single word, *parō*. Read with the class the Note on p. 104 and insist that the instructions must be followed. For a verb whose principal parts are given in full turn to p. 112.

Lesson 9, Section 3, p. 105. Emphasize the fact that, when the subject of a Latin verb is expressed in English, the pronoun is unnecessary in the translation. It is well to have students familiar with the idea that the Latin verb contains in its personal sign an indication of what English pronoun may be used, but guard against the tendency some students have to use the English pronoun always, as in "Mary she praises."

Purely formal drill on verbs should be brief. An immediate connection between form and meaning should be set up by proceeding quickly to the exercises. Simple oral exercise may be given by using typical sentences in which the subject can be changed from singular to plural, from first to second to third person.

Lesson 9, Section 4, p. 108. Help the students to analyze the new form, as shown in the four points on p. 109. Show the word written out both analytically *(laud - ā - ba - t)* and also as in the GRAMMAR *(laud -ābat)*. *Bā* is always the sign of the imperfect. If this is brought out clearly, the study of the other conjugations will be simplified.

In translating the imperfect tense students should consistently use the progressive forms as learned in the paradigm. Where awkward English results, permit the use of the past forms.

Lesson 9, Section 5, p. 112. Treat the future as you did the imperfect. Analyze the form: present stem, sign of the conjugation, tense sign, final personal sign. Note that *bi* is the tense sign for both the first and the second conjugations. When the future forms have been learned, you can begin using synopses as a form of exercise, calling for a certain form in each of the three tenses known; for example, third person plural, present, imperfect, and future indicative of *pugnō,* and so forth.

The principal parts of *dō* must be memorized as given.

Lesson 9, Section 6, p. 114. The use of pronouns is introduced very gradually. *Quid* has already appeared in the vocabulary, but was not identified as a pronoun. *Quis* and *quid* appear in this section identified as pronouns, but there is no suggestion that they are inflected forms. They are used here only in the nominative singular of the masculine and feminine and the nominative and accusative singular of the neuter. GR. 140 and 141 should not be studied here.

Lesson 9, Section 6, Exercise 129, p. 115. Call attention to the proper translation of *aliēnae* in sentence 8 and to the use of *aliēnus* for "another's" in sentence 6 of the following exercise.

Lesson 9, Section 7, p. 117. The *Glōria Patrī* as given on p. 118 should be assigned for memory work and used occasionally in class prayers. Try having students take turns leading the Latin prayers at the opening of class.

After the completion of this section return, if time permits, to the exercises on pp. 106 and 107 and use them for review lessons by asking Latin questions based on them. This same method may be used at any time in the future to give variety and to review the forms. Latin sentences assigned for translation may be made the subject of a quiz through Latin questions. It is good to insist on complete Latin sentences in answers to such questions.

Lesson 10, p. 120. The conjugation of the present system active of *moneō* is presented here on the basis of its similarity to the first conjugation. The long *ē* of the infinitive identifies *moneō* as being of the second conjugation and distinguishes it from verbs of the other conjugations. Follow the plan of the book in having students work out the conjugation as suggested on p. 121. The effort required of the student to do this helps to impress the matter deeply. You might further require him to write out the meanings of each form without consulting the GRAMMAR.

Lesson 10, Exercise 143, p. 124. Let the student discover how many of the words of his vocabulary can be used to complete the sentences and to describe the pictures. After a student has suggested one word, ask whether other words could also be used.

Lesson 11, Section 1, p. 125. Students find pronominal inflections much more difficult to retain than noun declensions. Drill them on pronouns whenever possible. Moreover, unless they master the pronouns introduced in the first year, they are almost sure to be hopelessly confused in the maze of personal, possessive, reflexive, relative, interrogative, intensive, and demonstrative pronouns they will be expected to use in the second year. Drill with them until they really understand each type of pronoun as it comes up.

In learning the declension of the personal pronouns students should add after the ablative the special forms *mēcum, tēcum, nōbīscum,* and *vōbīscum;* for example, *ego, meī, mihi, mē, mē, mēcum.* The same may be done later with *quōcum, quācum, quōcum,* and *quibuscum* when the relative pronoun is studied in Lesson 24.

Lesson 11, Section 1, Exercise 145, p. 126. This letter might be the basis of an exercise in Latin questions and answers. This will involve changing the person of many of the verbs throughout the exercise and will therefore be good practice in verb forms. For example, the first question might be, *"Ubi nunc est Mārcus?"*

Lesson 11, Section 1, Exercise 146, p 127. A word of warning should be added here. It is not the usual practice in Latin to express the pronominal subjects of verbs, and it is done here only as an exercise in pronouns.

Lesson 11, Section 2, p. 128. The fact that Latin uses a different form in the singular and plural for the pronoun of the second person, whereas English has the single form "you," should of course be emphasized.

The use of *neque* in the meaning "and . . . not" should be illustrated by a simple English sentence. The "and . . . not" may be meaningless and confusing unless you ask what conjunction would be used in such sentences as "I am not warning him and I will not warn him."

Imperātor is introduced here for review with an additional meaning, "emperor." Review vocabularies will appear from time to time to bring to the fore certain words already learned that may be used in the new constructions being taught.

Lesson 11, Section 2, Exercise 148, p. 129. Try dramatizing this in the classroom. Such an activity helps to show students that Latin is truly a language.

Lesson 11, Section 3, p. 132. The masculine and feminine forms of *is, ea, id* present no difficulty. The neuter form requires more attention.

Review the meaning of the term "pronoun." A noun is the name of a thing, *pro* means "in place of," therefore "pronoun" means "in the place of a noun." Logically, therefore, a pronoun has the same gender and number as the noun it stands for. The case, however, is determined by its use in the sentence. For example, "The bridge was captured by the Romans. They burned it." "It" stands for the bridge; it is therefore masculine singular. "It" is the direct object in the sentence and is therefore accusative. Note that these pronouns are ordinarily not used in Latin unless the noun for which they stand occurs in the previous sentence.

Lesson 11, Section 3, Exercise 152, p. 134. Sentence 9 requires special care in translating "it": as it refers to camp, *castra,* it must be neuter plural in Latin. This exercise and the preceding one may be returned to later for review of pronouns.

Lesson 11, Section 4, p. 135. Three points that will be helpful in teaching this new matter are the following: (1) A reflexive never has a nominative form, as it refers back to a subject. It cannot therefore *be* a subject, or occur in the nominative case. (2) A reflexive pronoun can never be dropped from a sentence without destroying either the structure or the meaning of the sentence; for example, "I see myself." Dropping "myself" destroys the meaning of this sentence, as "I see" means something different from "I see myself." (3) The forms of the personal pronouns *ego, nōs, tū,* and *vōs,* are used as the direct reflexive pronouns in the first and second persons, except that the nominative form is dropped. Note that the paradigms in GR. 123 and 124 give the reflexive meanings in the last column. It may be helpful to have students write "reflexive" in their grammars above this column of meanings.

There is a tendency among students to consider *suī* the only reflexive because of the frequency of occurrence of the third person. Point out that the GRAMMAR shows separately reflexive and nonreflexive forms only in the third person because in the first and second persons the reflexive and nonreflexive forms are identical.

Illustrate by means of simple sentences the difference in meaning between reflexive and nonreflexive pronouns. The examples on

p. 137 should be carefully explained and thoroughly understood. These examples make it clear that the translation of a reflexive pronoun is determined by the word to which it refers. This is especially important in the singular forms, as English has a different form for each gender.

A chart prepared in the following manner will help to clarify the two types of pronouns:

	PERSONAL PRONOUN (Subject)	VERB	REFLEXIVE PRONOUN (Object)
First Person	I *Ego*	fear *timeō*	myself. *mē.*
Second Person	You *Tū*	fear *timēs*	yourself. *tē.*
Third Person	He, She, It *Is, Ea, Id*	fears *timet*	himself, herself, itself. *sē.*
First Person	We *Nōs*	fear *timēmus*	ourselves. *nōs.*
Second Person	You *Vōs*	fear *timētis*	yourselves. *vōs.*
Third Person	They *Eī, Eae, Ea*	fear *timent*	themselves. *sē.*

Lesson 12, Section 1, p. 140. Throughout the study of the verb greater stress in practice should be placed on the third-person forms.[1] In this conjugation the principal parts require great emphasis, as there is no general rule for their formation. The principal parts of every third-conjugation verb in the vocabularies must be memorized.

Lesson 12, Section 2, p. 140. In commenting on the vocabulary, explain the notation "w. *bellum.*"

---

[1] Fifty-five per cent of all verb forms which occur in standard Latin authors are represented by only eight forms, namely: the present indicative active, third person singular and plural; the present infinitive, active and passive; the perfect indicative active, third person singular and plural; and the present and perfect participles. These statistics are based on a study of all the inflectional forms found in selections totaling 22,546 words, taken from Caesar, Cicero, Virgil, Ovid, Livy, and Nepos. A report on this study was presented by William H. Durand at the Illinois Classical Conference held in Springfield, Illinois, December 19, 1938.

Considerable drill is necessary before the forms of *mittō* are mastered, especially those of the present and future tenses. Students must memorize the principal parts of the verbs given in vocabularies, as the model verb *mittō* is of little help so far as principal parts are concerned.

Lesson 12, Section 2, Exercise 159, p. 142. This may serve the better students as a model for original short stories. Students with the necessary skill in drawing might be asked to portray the story in this exercise in a series of pictures.

Lesson 12, Section 3, p. 143. Make the most of the resemblance between *mittō* and *moneō* in the imperfect tense. No new explanations are necessary.

Lesson 12, Section 4, p. 145. Expand the statement given in the text as follows: (1) The sign of the future tense in the first and second conjugations is *bi*. There is no such sign in the future tense of the third conjugation. (2) The vowel of the ending changes. The endings in the first two conjugations have *i*: *-ābis, -ābit, -ēbis, -ēbit*, and so forth. The vowel of the ending in the future tense of the third conjugation is *e* except in the first person singular. (3) The personal signs remain the same: *-m, -s, -t, -mus, -tis, -nt*. (4) The form may be broken down as in the GRAMMAR:

STEM	ENDING (vowel + personal sign)
mitt	*-ēs*

Lesson 13, p. 147. All three tenses are seen immediately. Students can work out the paradigms by following the suggestions given. The little variations in this conjugation from the forms they already know are not difficult to comprehend, but considerable practice may be necessary before mastery results. Exercise 173 may be used as a drill on forms by requiring students to translate specific words without translating the entire sentence.

The Note on p. 147 is an opportunity for the teacher to see that students know the meaning of "transitive" and "intransitive."

Lesson 13, Exercise 174, p. 150. Call attention to the footnote if this exercise is used, especially in regard to the number of the verb. You might also write SPQR on the blackboard and keep it there for some time. What is the equivalent abbreviation for the United States?

Lesson 14, Section 1, p. 151. The appearance of *sum* as a complete conjugation has been delayed to this point so that the student's first formal acquaintance with the Latin verb might be with the regular conjugations. It is now taken up to prepare for study of the passive voice. The forms of the present tense have been known since the first unit, when predicate nouns were explained. Students should be reminded frequently that all forms of *sum* take the predicate noun.

The Assignment is important, as the smooth and speedy translation of the exercises requires some review of adjectives.

Lesson 15, Section 1, p. 155. The new matter to be learned is simple to comprehend, but memorizing and much practice will nevertheless be necessary.

All Latin verbs, regular and irregular, form the perfect tenses by adding a single set of endings to the perfect stem. There is really only one conjugation in the perfect system. When the formation of this tense is known for one conjugation, it is known for all. For this reason it is possible to cover the perfect system active of all the conjugations in a single lesson.

Lesson 15, Section 2, p. 155. The perfect indicative active is of basic importance. It is very common in Caesar, as Caesar is writing an historical report. Of all the forms of this tense, as of others, the third person singular and plural appear most frequently.

Lesson 15, Section 2, Exercise 181, p. 157. This exercise can be made very interesting and dramatic, and at the same time will serve to inculcate Christian principles.

Lesson 15, Section 3, p. 160. The future perfect is of slight importance in high-school Latin. Students should be required to know the paradigm as assigned on p. 161, but the exercises do not make use of the forms at this point.

Work Sheets for Written and Oral Drills

1. PARSING. For homework or for seatwork in class the teacher can mimeograph a sufficient number of copies of the work sheet

shown below. The words in the first column can either be dictated or, preferably, copied by the students from a list written on the blackboard. These words will of course change from day to day. Ruling the work sheet into rectangles will improve it.

VERB	PERSON	NUMBER	TENSE	MOOD	VOICE	TRANSLATION
petēbant						
audiam						
they will warn						
you (pl.) saw						
we conquered, and so forth						

2. SUPPLYING REQUIRED FORMS IN WRITING. The work sheet given below can be reproduced and supplied to students for written work. If possible, the names of the tenses should be spelled out in full, and not abbreviated as is done here because of the limitations of space. The work sheet may be ruled into rectangles, or lines may be supplied on which the forms are to be written. "Missing" may be typed in for forms that do not exist (for example, the future subjunctive), or students may be instructed either to leave the spaces blank or to indicate that the forms are missing by an X or a line. The verb to be used and the form required (for example, the third person plural) must be made known. This work sheet can economically be reproduced shortly after work on the verb has begun, as it is a simple matter to tell students how much of it they are required to fill out.

	PRES.	IMPERF.	FUT.	PERF.	PLUPF.	FUT. PERF.
ACTIVE						
Indicative						
Subjunctive						
Imperative						
Infinitive						
Participle						
Gerund						
PASSIVE						
Indicative						
Subjunctive						
Imperative						
Infinitive						
Participle						
Gerundive						

3. A CHART FOR RAPID ORAL DRILL. The following chart may be reproduced in large lettering to be hung in the front of the room or may be mimeographed to be given to each student. It contains the six tenses of the indicative and the four tenses of the subjunctive, and therefore cannot be used as it stands until Unit Eight has been completed. If it is used before that time, students can be told to skip forms not yet studied; or the chart could be rearranged so that the forms occur in lines or in columns in the order in which they are to be studied.

Drill may be on some one word made known by the teacher, or each student may be required to take the next word from a list written on the blackboard or supplied in mimeographed form. Students must be told whether drill is on the active voice or the passive voice. Note that in the chart as given each form occurs six times and is not repeated in any line or in any column.

perf. indic.	plupf. indic.	pres. indic.	pres. subj.	imperf. indic.	fut. indic.
pres. subj.	fut. indic.	perf. indic.	imperf. subj.	perf. subj.	pres. indic.
plupf. indic.	plupf. subj.	perf. subj.	imperf. indic.	fut. perf. indic.	perf. indic.
imperf. indic.	perf. indic.	fut. indic.	perf. subj.	pres. subj.	plupf. subj.
perf. subj.	fut. perf. indic.	plupf. indic.	pres. indic.	imperf. subj.	imperf. indic.
fut. indic.	pres. indic.	imperf. subj.	fut. perf. indic.	plupf. indic.	perf. subj.
plupf. subj.	imperf. subj.	pres. subj.	perf. indic.	fut. indic.	plupf. indic.
pres. indic.	imperf. indic.	fut. perf. indic.	fut. indic.	plupf. subj.	pres. subj.
fut. perf. indic.	pres. subj.	imperf. indic.	plupf. subj.	pres. indic.	imperf. subj.
imperf. subj.	perf. subj.	plupf. subj.	plupf. indic.	perf. indic.	fut. perf. indic.

Unit Four

This unit returns to nouns and adjectives, presenting a few that differ from those already learned. Throughout the unit continuous practice is given in the use of the active indicative tenses. Formal drill on these paradigms should be continued, as students should be very familiar with the active forms before they take up the passive forms in the following unit.

Lesson 16, Section 1, p. 163. These nouns should be taught with immediate dependence on *servus*. The text tells students to complete the declensions for themselves after the first two forms have been given. The teacher will do well if he constantly follows suggestions such as the one given here, for it cannot be said too often that active student participation in the development of a new step is most valuable.

Lesson 16, Section 3, p. 173. Occasionally a student is confused at first by the fact that these words *agree* with one word and *refer* to another. The examples given for agreement and usage should be analyzed and explained before any exercises are assigned. Show that, just as each personal pronoun has its own reflexive pronoun, so it has its own possessive adjective. The following example (completed for the plural if so desired) may be written on the blackboard.

	PERSONAL PRONOUN (Subject)	VERB	POSSESSIVE PRONOUN	
First	I	fear	my	friends.
Person	*Ego*	*timeō*	*meōs*	*amīcōs.*
Second	You	fear	your	friends.
Person	*Tu*	*timēs*	*tuōs*	*amīcōs.*
Third	He, She, It	fears	his, her, its	friends.
Person	*Is, Ea, Id*	*timet*	*suōs*	*amīcōs.*

Unit Five

Lesson 17, Section 2, p. 180. It will encourage students to hear that in learning the forms of the passive voice they are doing hardly more than reviewing the whole present system active, the only difference being the different personal signs that distinguish active from passive, somewhat as in the English: He is praising. He is praised. Recall the refrain, "To learn Latin, learn endings."

Some teachers believe that most of the errors in the translation or parsing of verbs are failures to recognize voice, chiefly through carelessness. Often the exact meaning of a sentence is lost because students fail to distinguish clearly and quickly between the active and the passive. This inaccuracy often results from ignorance of voice in English. If you consistently require students to identify voice first, this carelessness is generally overcome.

Lesson 17, Section 3, p. 181. Although it is sufficient for students to know that *laudāberis* is an exception, as the textbook states, it will be helpful for the teacher to know that *laudābis* becomes *laudāberis* because Latin does not admit of a short *i* before a medial *r* and that this *i* regularly becomes a short *e*.[1] This vowel change recurs in the present passive of the third conjugation.

Lesson 17, Section 4, p. 185. This construction opens up countless possibilities of drill on nouns, adjectives, and verbs. Students are sometimes helped by the "PPP" device in studying this construction: Verb must be in PASSIVE voice; agent must be a PERSON; *ab (ā)* must be the PREPOSITION.

Lesson 17, Section 4, Exercise 210, p. 187. This exercise may be used for sight translation. Allow four or five minutes of silent concentration. Ask one student to give in his own words the ideas contained in the passage, then ask another to translate exactly.

Lesson 17, Section 4, Exercise 213, p. 190. This exercise may be reserved for honor students, for even to them it will be a challenge. You will be surprised and gratified at their success in such tests of their mastery.

Lesson 19, Reading No. 9, p. 200. The name Scipio in this reading can be the occasion of an explanation of Roman names:

praenōmen	nōmen	cognōmen	second cognōmen or agnōmen
(given name)	*(name of gēns or clan)*	*(family name)*	*(name given in honor of achievements)*
Pūblius	Cornēlius	Scīpiō	Africānus

[1] Charles E. Bennett, *The Latin Language*, p. 97, No. 75, 1.

Lesson 20, Section 2, p. 203. After explaining the ablative of accompaniment, run through the exercises; but instead of having the entire sentence translated, simply require students to tell whether each "with" indicates means or accompaniment, and why. It will then be an easier matter to translate the entire sentence quickly and smoothly.

Lesson 21, p. 208. This lesson completes the development of the verb in its indicative forms. Considerable drill will probably be necessary before students master the passive forms of the perfect system. There is a tendency, especially in regard to the perfect tense, to translate the forms of *sum* in the present tense. *Laudātus sum* does not mean "I am praised" but "I was praised." Insist on the fact that any verb form containing a perfect participle must be translated by a past tense.

Unit Six

In this unit the student begins the study of the subjunctive and its use in the three types of purpose clauses: with *ut (nē)*, with *quī, quae, quod,* and with *quō (nē)* before a comparative. Relative clauses with the indicative are also introduced in this unit, and form a bridge to the relative purpose clause.

Students, if they remember their English grammar, know that the subjunctive in English expresses a wish, a desire, a purpose, an uncertainty, or a condition contrary to fact. They will discover that the subjunctive is used in Latin when there is no element of uncertainty, contingency, or subjectivity. For this reason some teachers distinguish between Latin subjunctives which they call *true* subjunctives and others which they call *constructional* subjunctives. If you are sure of your ground and if you have a class brilliant enough to follow you, there may be profit in discussions such as these. The text, however, contents itself with saying that the subjunctive is sometimes used in Latin when we would not use it in English. For the average student it is enough if he knows this fact and learns his rules.

Lesson 22, Section 1, p. 225. There is little to be done here except to memorize the subjunctive forms. Pages 48 and 49 of the GRAMMAR are so arranged that the four conjugations can be seen together, and their differences noted. It may be said that the vowels characteristic of the various conjugations appear in the present infinitive; the changes for the present subjunctive are:

	I	II	III	IV
Present infinitive	ā	ē	e	ī
Present subjunctive	e	ea	a	ia

Lesson 22, Section 2, p. 226. The explanation given in the text should be sufficient, but it will help to have the sentence written on the blackboard as the analysis is explained.

When working out Exercise 242, have students not only follow the four suggested steps but name the kind of subordinate clause (purpose) and the introductory word *(ut)*. A written analysis may take the following form:

1. *Castra vallō mūnit ut ea dēfendat* is a complex sentence. *Castra vallō mūnit* is the main clause. *Ut ea dēfendat* is the subordinate clause. (When clauses are long have students give only the introductory word and the verb in the main clause and the subordinate clause; for example, *ut . . . dēfendat.*)

2. The subordinate clause is introduced by *ut; dēfendat* is in the subjunctive mood.

3. The subordinate clause answers the question why and is therefore an adverbial clause. It gives the purpose of the action described in the main clause and is therefore a purpose clause.

4. After sequence of tenses has been taught another step may be added, as follows: *Mūnit,* the verb of the main clause, is present tense, *dēfendat* is present subjunctive. The sentence is therefore in primary sequence.

Lesson 22, Section 3, p. 228. In explaining this section it is not advisable to explain the whole organization of tense sequence. The need for this information does not arise until indirect questions are studied in Lesson 26. Since purpose clauses are restricted to the present and the imperfect tenses of the subjunctive, a limited amount of information regarding sequence is necessary and useful. It will be sufficient to say that when a subordinate clause in Latin takes the subjunctive mood, the tense of the subjunctive is determined by a pattern or arrangement known as "sequence." Of this pattern we need know only two points for purpose clauses:

1. The present, future, and future perfect tenses in the indicative are called *primary* tenses.

2. When the main verb is in a primary tense, use the *present* subjunctive in the purpose clause.

Emphasize the point that purpose clauses may be expressed by infinitives in English, and most frequently are, but this is not done in Latin. If this point needs detailed explanation, this might be made in the following way:

1. Write the sentence on the blackboard: He is fighting to defend the city.

2. What question does the phrase "to defend the city" answer? It answers the question why.

3. It therefore tells the purpose of the action described in the main verb. The phrase expresses purpose.

4. What part of speech is "to defend"? An infinitive.

5. In Latin we cannot express purpose by an infinitive. What must we do? We must change this infinitive to a clause. When we do so, we have a complex sentence, the subordinate clause of which expresses purpose. A purpose clause, our rule says, is introduced by *ut* (in order that). The verb in the purpose clause is put in the subjunctive.

6. Our second rule tells us what tense to use in the subordinate clause: When the main verb is in a primary tense, use the present subjunctive in the purpose clause.

Lesson 22, Section 4, p. 230. Do not be surprised if you have to explain negative purpose and the conjunction "lest" rather carefully. Some students cannot immediately distinguish negative clauses from positive.

Students should be cautioned not to confuse the introductory word *nē* with the enclitic *-ne* learned previously for use in questions. Sentences 1 and 2 of Exercise 246 illustrate the two words.

Stress the point raised in the Note on Translation, p. 232. It is of great importance that students exercise a certain freedom in translating words from Latin to English. Always encourage the use of other meanings than those appearing in the vocabularies when this is necessary to attain good sense, better idiom, or more vivid expression. *Altus*, for example, may be "lofty," "steep," "tall," or "towering" in the first sentence given under the Note.

Exercise 250 is an important review of many of the points learned up to this lesson. This review is not confined to the italicized words. There are other notable points in some of the sentences to which attention may be called.

Sentence 1. *veniunt*, 3rd pl. present, fourth-conjugation verb; *ut . . . videant*, purpose clause, second-conjugation verb.

Sentence 2. *et . . . et*, "both . . . and."

Sentence 6. *cum mīlitibus*, ablative of accompaniment.

Sentence 7. *vallō et fossā*, ablative of means; *mūniuntur*, 3rd pl. present passive, fourth-conjugation verb; *nē . . . expugnent*, negative purpose clause, first-conjugation verb.

Sentence 8. *grātiās agunt*, idiom; *mīlitibus*, indirect object.

Sentence 9. *Suntne*, interrogative particle.

Lesson 23, p. 235. This lesson covers the imperfect subjunctive forms, identifies the secondary tenses, and introduces adjectives used as nouns.

Lesson 23, Section 2, p. 237. Remind students of the discussion on primary tenses in the previous lesson. Here again only a small portion of the subject of sequence is introduced. It is enough to identify the secondary tenses, and to present the rule that, if the main verb is in one of the secondary tenses, we use the imperfect subjunctive in the purpose clause.

Note that in translating purpose clauses following a secondary tense the word "might" is used. That "might" is the past form of "may" is not always realized by students.

Lesson 23, Section 3, p. 241. In commenting on the vocabulary do not fail to call attention to the note on the gender of *obses*.

Idiom Study should be introduced with a short explanation. Some students do not know what "idiom" means.

Lesson 24, p. 246. This lesson takes up the very important question of the relative pronoun and its use in clauses, especially the relative clause of purpose. The third type of purpose clause is also included, and lessons on the use of the preposition *ad*.

Lesson 24, Section 1, p. 246. Do not take for granted students' knowledge of the relative pronoun in English. The material on pp. 246 and 247 should be thoroughly covered. It may be helpful to add certain other points:

1. A relative clause can occur only in a complex sentence. The text says this when it says that a relative pronoun introduces a subordinate adjective clause.

2. This pronoun is called "relative" because it relates to someone or something. This someone or something is called the antecedent of the pronoun. The word "antecedent" is derived from two Latin words, *ante*, "before," and *cēdō*, "go."

3. The rules of agreement are the same as those for personal pronouns as learned in Lesson 11 and GR. 479.

4. It may be necessary to emphasize that "who" is a nominative form only. The incorrect use of "who" for "whom" is a common error. This point is important in translating relative clauses.

Relative clauses may cause more difficulty than purpose clauses, indirect questions, and other clauses requiring the subjunctive. Much earnest practice is necessary before students arrive at mastery over these constructions.

Call for a complete analysis as long as this is necessary; for example, take the sentence: Caesar, whom I saw in Gaul, is a great general.

This is a complex sentence. The main or independent clause is "Caesar is a great general."

The subordinate clause is "whom I saw in Gaul."

"Whom" is the relative pronoun, masculine singular because its antecedent is "Caesar"; accusative because it is the direct object in its own clause.

After the English essentials have been reviewed, the Latin forms of the relative pronoun are taught. Certain forms require special attention: *quem; quibus;* and *quae,* which occurs both in the feminine, nominative singular and plural, and in the neuter, nominative and accusative plural.

In showing how the Latin pronouns are to be translated, note that "who" and "which" may be used in both restrictive and non-restrictive clauses, but "that" only in restrictive clauses:

Christ, who is the Son of God, was killed by the Romans.
The legions which (that) Caesar was leading into the province had been recently conscripted.
This legion, which had just recently come into the province, was fighting in the forest.

Notice the gradation in Exercises 263 to 265. In the first, students are asked only to supply one form of the relative. For this, concentration on the Latin form is required. In the second, translation is required but the italics give a clue to the relative clause. In the third, translation from English to Latin is required. In preparation for this exercise it may be helpful to call for analysis of the English forms and for the correct Latin forms. An outline such as the following may be used:

	RELATIVE	ANTECEDENT	GENDER	NUMBER	CASE	LATIN FORM
Sentence 1	who	slaves	masculine	plural	nom.	*quī*
Sentence 9	which	legions	feminine	plural	dat.	*quibus*

If these three exercises are carefully and conscientiously done by each student, mastery will not be far off.

Lesson 24, Section 3, p. 258. Purpose clauses with *ut* and the subjunctive being quite fresh in students' minds it will be useful to give an example of such a sentence. Although the text offers five English translations for *quī cōnsilia cognōscerent*, it may be necessary to analyze this in more detail. Write your English sentence on the blackboard: He sent cavalry to learn the plans.

Ask students to point out the main clause, to identify the idea of purpose, and to name the phrase by which this idea is expressed ("to learn"). Remind them that this must be changed to a clause in order to be translated into Latin. Now point out that the clauses beginning "that," "in order that," and "in order to," such as they learned a few lessons back, are not the only kind of clause that the English infinitive expressing purpose may be changed to. Another way to change the English before translating is shown in sentence 2 on p. 258, where a relative clause is used.

Exercise 273 requires students to identify the sentences that may be translated by a relative clause of purpose. It may be helpful to emphasize the following facts in connection with the use of a relative clause of purpose in place of the *ut*-clause.

1. The only difference in the Latin construction is the substitution of a relative pronoun for *ut* as the introductory word in the subordinate purpose clause; the rules for mood and tense which were taught in connection with the *ut*-clause apply in exactly the same way to the relative clause.

2. The relative clause is preferable to the *ut*-clause and should be substituted for the *ut*-clause whenever possible.

3. The exception to the general rule mentioned on page 258 is very important. A relative clause cannot be used if the introductory relative pronoun would have to agree with the subject of an *active* main verb. (The relative pronoun can agree with the subject of a *passive* main verb. See Sentence 2 in Exercise 273.)

Lesson 24, Section 4, p. 263. The third type of purpose clause is relatively simple. When this has been covered students are responsible for the three types, and the complete rule, GR. 546, should be memorized.

In commenting on the vocabulary, give special attention to *appropinquō.*. This is the first example of a verb taking a dative other than dative of indirect object.

The Note on Translation is very important. Do not tolerate slovenly translations or unidiomatic expressions. Good sense and good English are the twin goals. It may be well at this point also to bring up again the subject of reading for comprehension in the Latin order. Constant practice on this from the beginning, when sentences are short, will be an invaluable aid to mastery and a good preparation for more advanced Latin. Much help can be found in *On Reading and Translating Latin,* by Hugh P. O'Neill and William R. Hennes (Loyola University Press, 1929).

Unit Seven

Lesson 25, Section 1, p. 267. If, before beginning the exercises, it seems necessary to drive home the difference betwen *ubi* and *quō,* you can ask qustions such as the following: (1) Which would you use, *ubi* or *quō,* if you were asking someone where he is? Where he is going? Where he is hiding? Where he is hastening? Where he is studying? and so forth. (2) Why can you not use *ubi* with the word "hurrying"? *Quō* with the word "eating"? and so forth. (3) Sometimes we could use· either *ubi* or *quō* with the same verb, but with a different meaning. If I ask where you are running, what would be the difference between the same question with *ubi* and with *quō?* (I am running in the stadium; I am running to the river.) Explain that "rest in" a place does not mean that the subject is absolutely motionless. The subject may be running, but he is represented as running *in some place,* not *toward some place.*

Lesson 25, Section 2, p. 271. Where rules are called for, as in Exercise 285, the exact wording that has been taught should be required. The two rules mentioned here are Gr. 546 and 479.

Lesson 25, Section 3, p. 272. A few more examples may be given to clarify the use of *trāns* and *trādūcō,* as follows: He led the legion across the bridge, across a desert, across the province. The preposition *trāns* has already been learned and used in sentences with *dūcō.* It will be natural enough for students to use *trāns* with *trādūcō,* and the new point to be noted here is that since *trādūcō* already contains the notion of "across" the accusative without a preposition may also be used to express the thing over which the direct object is led.

Lesson 25, Section 4, p. 274. The distinction between *quis* and *quī* for the nominative masculine singular need not be memorized here. It is a point of style not used at this time but occurring later in the series. To help students distinguish between the interrogative pronoun and the interrogative adjective show various examples both in English and in Latin, as follows: Who is the leader? Which leader set out for Gaul? What is your name? What name did you give your dog? *Quis est rēx? Quis rēx bellum gessit? Ad quōs litterās mīsit? Ad quōs lēgātōs litterās mīsit?*

Lesson 25, Section 4, Exercise 291, p. 276. The answers to the Quiz on American History are as follows: (1) Attack on Pearl

Harbor. (2) Paul Revere. (3) George Washington. (4) France. (5) General Douglas MacArthur. (6) War of 1812. (7) Thomas Jonathan Jackson. (8) Jolliet and Marquette.

Lesson 26, Section 2, p. 281. The concept of indirect questions will not be difficult if you show a number of examples of direct questions changed to indirect in the manner of the two examples given in the text. Among these should be some using interrogative pronouns, adjectives, and adverbs, as well as those introduced by *-ne* and *num:* Who is the general? I ask who the general is. Where are we? I ask where we are. How many legions are fighting? I ask how many legions are fighting. It is sufficient at this time to use only verbs of asking, as in the textbook, although verbs of saying, thinking, and the like all take this construction.

It will be noticed that the question of sequence has not been directly presented up to this time. In the study of purpose clauses only the distinction between primary and secondary tenses was taught; nothing further was necessary, as the primary tenses could there be followed only by the present subjunctive, the secondary tenses only by the imperfect subjunctive. Now the general rule is presented and assigned for memorization (GR. 524-526), but the more detailed treatment given in GR. 527-533 is not offered to the class. It must be remembered that the GRAMMAR contains the essential grammatical material for a four-year course. Teach only as much as the textbook indicates. The two diagrams (GR. 536 and 537) may be reproduced on the blackboard with the portion titled "after" omitted or set off in brackets. Two hints which may prove helpful are the following: The main verb determines the *sequence* (primary or secondary). The verb of the subordinate clause and its time relation to the main verb determine the *tense* of the subjunctive.

Explain that the term "sequence" is derived from the verb *sequor,* follow. The rules of primary sequence tell us what tenses of the subjunctive may follow main verbs that are in the primary tenses, and the rules of secondary sequence tell us what tenses may follow main verbs that are in the secondary tenses. It is important for students to have a clear idea of what the word means.

Lesson 26, Section 3, Note, p. 287. *Inquit* is always used with direct quotations. It is never used with quotations indirectly expressed (accusative with infinitive construction). But direct quotations may be introduced by other words, such as *dīxit, respondit, sic locūtus est,* and so forth.

Lesson 26, Section 3, Exercise 303, p. 290. For the benefit of those who have not leased a key we repeat here the answers to Exercise 303 as given in the key. 1. Direct questions are introduced by (1) interrogative pronouns, adjectives, and adverbs; (2) *nōnne* if the answer yes is expected; (3) *num* if the answer no is expected or to express surprise; (4) *-ne* to ask for information. The indicative mood is used. (See Gr. 503.) 2. *Ubi* can be used only when "where" refers to place in which and implies rest; *quō* can be used only when "where" refers to place to which and implies motion or direction. 3. *-Ne* is used to ask for information; *num* when the answer no is expected or to express surprise; *nōnne* when the answer yes is expected. For example: Vīdistīne Rōmam? Num Caesar victus est? Nōnne Deus est bonus? Caesar wasn't conquered, was he? Surely Caesar wasn't conquered? God is good, isn't He? Is not God good? 4. See Gr. 140. It is a pronoun because it stands in place of a noun. 5. See Gr. 141. 6. *Quis* is used as an adjective for *which* or *what* in the nominative masculine singular. (See text, p. 274.) 7. *Quī* is used for *quis* to express *what sort of, what kind of.* (See text, p. 274.) It is also used sometimes for *quis* in indirect questions. (See text, p. 282.) 8. With verbs of transporting the thing over which the direct object is led is put in the accusative without a preposition or with *trāns.* (See text, p. 272.) 9. Verbs of calling, naming, making, showing, etc., may take two accusatives, one of the direct object, the other a predicate accusative. When *nōmen* is used, *nōmen* is in the ablative. (See text, p. 275.) 10. See Gr. 200-207. The perfect active stem is used. 11. Indirect questions are those which depend on a verb of asking, saying, thinking, and the like. 12. The mood in indirect questions is always subjunctive. They are introduced by *-ne* and *num* (meaning *whether, if*); occasionally by *nōnne;* by *quī* sometimes for *quis.* 13. See answer 12 above and text, p. 282. 14. *Quī* is sometimes used for *quis*. (See text, p. 282.) 15. See GR. 525-541 and text, pp. 282, 286. 16. *Inquit* means *he says* or *he said;* it is used in direct quotations and is placed after the first word or words of the quotation. 17. Examples of the four tenses will be found in sentences 1 and 2 of Exercise 296, p. 283, and sentences 1 and 2 of Exercise 299, p. 287.

Unit Eight

Lesson 27, Section 2, p. 296. Mention, if you wish, that there is a future imperative, not taught because it is rarely used: *estō fortis, estōte fortēs.*

Lesson 27, Section 3, p. 300. The words "volitive" (sometimes "optative") and "hortatory" should be explained: *volō* (wish, am willing)—we wish *somebody else* to do it; *hortor* (urge, encourage)—we are encouraging *ourselves* to do it.

Lesson 28, p. 305. This is an important lesson. The textbook provides adequate practice on direct and indirect reflexives, but the explanation must be gone through very carefully, and its various points repeated at frequent intervals throughout the coming lessons. When taking Exercises 318, 321, and 322 orally, immediately following the grammatical explanation, demand full explanations of the italicized words. The "next section" to which reference is made on p. 305 is Section 2, p. 309.

Lesson 29, Section 2, p. 318. Explain "secondary sequence" once more if necessary. This is such an important notion for future work that it must be well established as early as possible. *Cum* always introduces a *subordinate* clause—subordinate to some *principal* clause. Pupils are already familiar with sequence of tenses in indirect questions and in purpose clauses, although the latter were limited to the present and the imperfect subjunctive. These subordinate *cum*-clauses are limited to the imperfect or the pluperfect subjunctive (secondary sequence). A few examples of primary sequence may be given in English, such as: When winter comes, can spring be far behind? When I go to Rome, I will see the pope. Do not offer any examples in Latin, however, as *cum*-clauses referring to present or future time take the indicative.

Unit Nine

Lesson 30, Note, p. 326. *Pugnō,* which the text gives as an example of an intransitive verb, is used transitively very rarely, and then only with a cognate accusative: *pugnāre pugnam.*

The student is instructed to review the ablative of cause. On p. 320 a few examples of the ablative of cause are given, and the statement is made that the ablative of cause is frequently difficult to distinguish from the ablative of means. In Exercises 338 and 339 the student is required to parse a number of ablatives, in connection with some of which the difficulty to which reference has been made may occur. For this reason it may help the teacher to have a somewhat fuller explanation.

The ablative of cause is used to indicate the cause or reason on account of which one is in a certain state or does a certain thing. *Victōriā gaudet,* He rejoices in his victory, is an example given in the GRAMMAR.

The ablative of means is used to indicate the nonliving agent, the means, or the instrument by which one brings about some desired result. *Collem vallō mūnīvit* contains an ablative of means concerning which there can be no difficulty or argument.

Sometimes, however, a person uses a certain means for the purpose of bringing about in another a state of mind because of which the other will be led to take some action. Take the expression *Gallī, adventū Caesaris commōtī.* If the meaning is simply this, that the Gauls were as a matter of fact alarmed by the arrival of Caesar, *adventū* should be parsed as an ablative of cause. If it is evident from the context that Caesar went where he did for the precise purpose of alarming the Gauls, *adventū* can be parsed as an ablative of means. Teachers frequently instruct students to parse such an ablative as "ablative of cause or of means." Such a method of parsing does not indicate ignorance of syntax, but rather a realization of the fact that either explanation could be defended in the context.

Lesson 30, Exercise 337, p. 327. The "two translations of the participle" that the student is required to give are, of course, "having been known" and "known," and so forth.

Lesson 32, Exercise 350, p. 338. The student is told to illustrate his translations with drawings or diagrams. The diagrams that the author has in mind will be similar to the one on p. 222 of the GRAMMAR.

Instead of having students draw diagrams in their written exercises, it might be more practical to instruct them to be ready to go to the blackboard and draw the diagrams. Whatever you decide to do, look over the exercise yourself and be ready with suggestions for expressions not covered by the diagram in the GRAMMAR; for example, into the water (sentence 1), across the river (sentence 2), at the river (sentence 5), in these battles (sentence 10).

Lesson 33, Note, p. 341. The note concerning the translation of *ratiō* is intended as remote preparation for work to come later, as the word is used or called for only a few times in the present lesson. *Dē bellī ratiōne* in the first sentence of Exercise 353 can be translated by "the manner of waging the war" or "the way in which the war should be waged." In your constant insistence on the use of pure and idiomatic English you can even at times ask students to suggest improvements in the English-Latin exercises, which had to be written in such a way that students could translate them without too much difficulty. Sentence 1 in Exercise 354 is not the kind of an English sentence that we would expect to hear or read; but *ratiō proeliī* could not be called for in an English-Latin exercise in any other way without creating too much difficulty for the student.

Lesson 34, Section 2, Exercise 360, p. 350. For the benefit of those who have not leased a key we repeat the answers to this exercise given in the key. 1. It is the fourth principal part of the verb. 2. (a) Soldiers encumbered by full packs; (b) army encumbered by a baggage train; (c) places difficult to maneuver. 3. Either as a pronoun or as the demonstrative adjective *this*. 4. As ablatives of place from which they are distinguished as follows: *ex*, the person moving is inside the place and goes out of it; *dē*, the person moving is inside or on the place and goes down from it; *ab*, the person moving is not inside the place. *Dē* and *ab* are also used in other types of ablatives. 5. *Ā* and *ē* may be used for *ab* and *ex* before words beginning with consonants; *ab* and *ex* before any letter, but rarely before *b, p, f, v,* and *m*. (See Gr. 932 and 958.) 6. For a complete answer see Gr. 792-798. 7. With verbs and adjectives of separating, freeing, depriving, and the like use the ablative without a preposition with things and the ablative with *dē, ex,* or *ab* with persons; e.g., *Metū līber sum; Ā tyrannīs pātriam līberāvī.* (See Gr. 766.)

Unit Ten

Lesson 35, Section 2, Reading No. 26, p. 358. Encourage students to suggest free and idiomatic translations. *Rēgēs quī imperium et rēgnum obtinent* can be translated "Kings who possess authority and royal power," *Tamen amīcitiam cōnfirmāre nōn potuit* can be translated "Despite all these efforts he could not bring Ratislaus to a friendly understanding," and so forth.

Lesson 35, Section 3, Note 2, p. 360. *Cōnsuēvī* as a transitive verb is rare. It is used in such expressions as "to accustom a bull to the yoke," and so forth.

Lesson 35, Section 4, Note, p. 364. Other good translations for *oportet (mē)* are "it is incumbent upon me," "it is my duty," "I have an obligation of," "I must."

Unit Eleven

Lesson 37, Section 1, p. 381. The rule given here for the endings of *-iō* verbs is helpful, and should be read and explained. The essential thing is for the students to learn the conjugation, which they can do without difficulty.

Lesson 37, Section 2, Exercise 386, p. 386. The answers are: (1) In 1492. (2) On Thanksgiving Day. (3) In 1863. (4) On Good Friday. (5) On the night of the Nativity. (6) On Ascension Thursday.

Lesson 37, Section 4, Exercise 397, p. 395. The answers are: (1) 2,470 miles. (2) 300 feet at St. Paul; 1,400 feet at mouth of Illinois River. (3) Rome to New York City, 4,273 miles. (4) Forty days. (5) Entire life, about 33 years; public life, probably two years and some months but commonly said to be three years. (6) 3 years, 10 months. (7) In World War I, 1 year, 7 months; in World War II, 3 years, 6 months.

Lesson 37, Section 5, Note, p. 399. You may mention that the passive of *faciō* is *fīō*, conjugated in GR. 366-368 and 381-385.

Lesson 37, Section 7, Exercise 407, p. 404. Students enjoy this exercise. The missing letters, which can easily be supplied without help, are as follows: line 1, *a, s;* line 2, *n;* line 5, *u;* line 6, *e;* line 7, *ent;* line 8, *s;* line 9, *e;* line 10, *ant;* line 11, *us;* line 14, *e;* line 15, *em;* line 16, *es;* line 19, *ia;* line 22, *a, c;* line 24, *a, is;* line 28, *en.*

Units Twelve, Thirteen, and Fourteen

Only superior classes will be able to cover these units which contain such important topics as: future, perfect, and passive infinitives; the accusative with the infinitive; comparison of adjectives; irregular adjectives; ablative of comparison; deponent verbs; and the irregular verb *eō.* All the constructions are presented again in the book for second year.

PART THREE: SECOND YEAR LATIN

SECOND YEAR LATIN is divided into four parts: Julius Caesar and Roman Imperialism (short historical background); Roman Imperialism in Gaul (simplified text of Caesar's *Gallic War*); Jesus Christus, Rex Regum (Christian Latin); and Exercises Based on Caesar. The teacher will begin the year's work by reviewing declensions, conjugations, points of grammar, and constructions that were studied in FIRST YEAR LATIN and laying the necessary foundation for the study of Caesar (Lessons 1-16). With Lesson 17 (page 395) the student begins the reading of Caesar. Every lesson thereafter has a definite reading assignment in Part II. The Christian Latin should not be neglected. Two selections are from the Mass of Christ the King (the last Sunday in October); selections for the Christmas season include "Adeste Fidelis," the adoration of the Magi, and a hymn for the Feast of the Holy Innocents. Other excerpts are taken from the New Testament, St. Augustine, and *The Following of Christ*.

Portions of the first, third, and fourth books of Caesar's *Gallic War* (The Helvetian Drive to the West, Revolt along the Seacoast, and The First Invasion of Britain) have been simplified and arranged for intensive study by all students. The fifth and seventh books (Rebellion in the North and All Gaul in Arms) are included for extensive reading, particularly by superior students.

LATIN PROGRESS TESTS, SECOND YEAR, provide objective-type exercises for each of the thirty-two lessons in the textbook. It is strongly recommended that teachers with large classes make use of this supplementary material. The work may be scored by students, either by exchanging papers or by letting each student correct his own work.

Lesson 1, p. 305. Grammar assignments in this lesson refer to: 45-64, gender and declension of nouns in the third declension; 346-351, conjugation of *sum* (indicative mood); 460-461, 469, order of words in Latin sentences; 470-473, agreement of verb and predicate noun with subject.

Reference should be made to the five Latin declensions, the cases, and the endings in the first and second declensions before beginning the study of the third declension. The lesson is devoted primarily to the third declension because this declension includes masculine, feminine, and neuter nouns, and the two types of genitive plural. After the lesson is completed, it would be advisable to include a rapid review of the fourth and fifth declensions. (The Sign of the Cross on page 308 presents an opportunity to introduce *Spīritus*.)

Lesson 1, p. 307. Before beginning Exercise 3 review the Latin prepositions learned in first year: *ab, cum, dē, ex, in, prō,* and *sine* with the ablatives; *ad, in, inter, per, post, propter,* and *trāns* with the accusative. If students have learned their vocabularies with all the "equipment" as suggested on page 8 of this manual, they will have no difficulty in determining the case that is to be used with any given preposition.

Exercises 4 and 5 stress the application of the rules of agreement and position. Attention may also be called to the personal pronouns, *ego* and *tū,* and the possessive adjective *noster.*

Lesson 2, p. 309. Grammar assignments refer to: 72-78, declension of adjectives (including those of the third declension in *-is, -is, -e*); 464-465, 474-478, position and agreement of adjectives.

Lesson 2, p. 310. Exercise 7 is a drill exercise; do not omit, for it furnishes a good review for the declension of nouns belonging to first, second, and fifth declensions as well as those of the third declension studied in Lesson 1. If desired, special cases rather than complete declensions may be requested. Call attention to the position of adjectives.

Lesson 2, p. 311. Review the adjectives governing cases that were studied in first year—*cupidus, finitimus, plēnus, similis*—before translating Exercises 10 and 11.

Lesson 2, p. 312. The note concerning translations is important. Suggest better English translations when you see that students are inclined to give liberal translations in awkward English. This admonition will probably have to be repeated frequently throughout the year.

Lesson 3, p. 314. Grammar assignments refer to: 160-185, 312-314, 321, indicative active of the four conjugations and of *-iō* verbs of the third; 140, declension of the interrogative pronoun; 502-503, direct questions.

The *-iō* verbs of the third conjugation will probably be new material for most classes, for they are not introduced until Unit Eleven of FIRST YEAR LATIN. It is therefore important to devote some time to a discussion of these verbs and to make certain that sufficient drill is given on their conjugation. The fact that in the first person singular these verbs look exactly like verbs of the fourth conjugation provides an opportunity to point out once more the necessity of learning the principal parts of all verbs. If time does not permit conjugating the *-iō* verbs completely in class, at least synopsize them with the class. To conjugate them completely does not take long if six students are sent to the board to conjugate an individual tense. At the same time the rest of the class can make a synopsis of a different *-iō* verb with the help of the teacher. This will prevent them from being distracted by what is being done at the board until this work is ready to be checked.

Lesson 3, p. 316. Note that all the sentences in Exercises 16 and 17 call for the use of interrogative pronouns, adverbs, or one of the particles. The explanation of the interrogative adjective should be deferred until later. (This form is taught on page 450, and the exercises there will give students the necessary drill.) Be sure that the declension of the interrogative pronoun is thoroughly mastered now so that students will not confuse this pronoun with the relative pronoun when it is introduced in Lesson 13.

Lesson 4, p. 320. Grammar assignments refer to: 186, 194-196, present subjunctive active of the four regular conjugations; 315, present subjunctive active of *-iō* verbs; 352, present subjunctive of *sum*. These conjugations should present no real difficulties, but much drill is necessary, particularly for those who failed to master the forms of the subjunctive mood in first year.

Three uses of the present subjunctive (all in principal clauses) receive attention in this lesson. The hortatory subjunctive (GR. 518) and the subjunctive with possible wishes (GR. 511) were introduced in Unit Eight of FIRST YEAR LATIN, but will not have been studied by all students; the use of the present subjunctive to express commands in the third person (GR. 514) is introduced here for the first time. A blackboard chart will help to point up the similarities and differences between these three types of subjunctives and help students to identify each construction.

	HORATORY	POSSIBLE WISHES	COMMANDS THIRD PERSON
Person	First	First, Second, Third	Third
Number	Plural	Singular, Plural	Singular, Plural
Tense and Mood	Pres. subj.	Pres. subj.	Pres. subj.
English Auxiliary	Let (us)	May	Let (them)
Latin Particle	....	Utinam (may be omitted in third person)	....
Negative	Nē	Nē	Nē

Lesson 4, p. 324. It may be helpful to tell students something about the inscriptions which were used by the early Christians. Supplementary information is readily available in the article entitled "Inscriptions" in the Catholic Encyclopedia. Perhaps some interested student could be asked to prepare a brief report. Although such digressions should not be permitted frequently because of the limited amount of time available, an occasional break in the regular routine will increase interest in Latin.

The questions at the end of the historical reading on page 326 will serve as a further review of direct questions as well as a quiz on the students' comprehension of the selection. Similar readings in English will occur at intervals throughout the book; they should not be omitted, for they give information that is valuable for a correct understanding of Caesar's campaigns in Gaul and his fighting forces.

Lesson 5, p. 328. Grammar assignments refer to: 187, 197-207, 316, 321, 353, 355-356, subjunctive active of the four regular conjugations, of -*iō* verbs of the third, and of *sum;* 524-528, 531-532, 535-537, sequence of tenses; 660-662, indirect questions.

Many students have difficulties with the indirect question. Discuss with the class the examples given here in which a direct question is changed to an indirect question. Stress the fact that these are complex sentences; there is a main clause and a subordinate noun clause (used as object of the verb in the main clause). A number of examples involving only the present indicative and the present subjunctive, perhaps some drills imitating model sentences, should be given to provide practice in this construction.

Model: *Quaerō ubi Caesar sit.*
I ask where Caesar is.

1. He asks where the lieutenant is.
2. They ask where the soldiers are.
3. I ask where you are.
4. Caesar knows where they are pitching camp.
5. You know where the troops are assembling.

Model: *Quaerō num Mariam laudētis.*
I ask whether you praise Mary.

6. You ask whether we praise Christ.
7. They ask whether we have grain.
8. Caesar asks whether the soldiers are guarding the bridge.
9. I ask whether the Romans are waging war.
10. You know whether you fear God.

When the majority of pupils understand indirect questions call attention to the fact that we may sometimes use another tense—I know where you *were;* they asked whether we *had seen* Rome. We have to learn other tenses of the subjunctive (GR. 197-207, 316, 321, 353, 355-356) before we can translate such sentences. Call attention to the easy way to remember the imperfect subjunctive: present infinitive + personal sign. Both the perfect and the pluperfect subjunctive are formed on the perfect stem; *eri* is the sign of the perfect subjunctive and *isse* the sign of the pluperfect subjunctive. These simple rules apply to all conjugations and to *sum.*

Sequence of tenses requires intensive study. See page 57 of this manual for suggestions. Go over the examples in GR. 662 slowly, analyzing each one. If students find it difficult to determine whether or not the verb in the subordinate clause indicates action prior to the time of the verb in the main clause, point out that prior action indicates completed action. If the action of the verb in the main clause is completed, either the perfect or the pluperfect subjunctive must be used in the indirect question. Frequently call the attention of the class to sequence of tenses in the Latin readings, especially when more difficult constructions are involved. The last two sentences in the reading on page 332 offer an excellent opportunity to compare sequence of tenses in two sentences which have the same structure.

Lesson 6, p. 335. Grammar assignments refer to: 123-126, personal pronouns of the first and second persons and possessive adjectives and pronouns of the first and second persons; 128-130, 132, non-reflexive personal pronouns of the third person and non-reflexive adjective and pronoun of the third person; 479, agreement of pronouns; 127, reflexive personal pronoun of the third person; 131, reflexive possessive adjective and pronoun of the third person; 800-804, syntax of reflexive pronouns.

The explanation of the use of *is, ea, id* as a pronoun in the third person will probably have to be repeated more than once. Students find it hard to understand that where the English translation calls for *it,* the Latin requires a masculine or feminine pronoun to agree with the antecedent. Additional examples requiring plural forms may be given:

The soldiers fought bravely. We praise them.
Mīlitēs fortiter pugnāvērunt. Eōs laudāmus.
The legions arrived at the camp. Caesar had led them.
Legiōnēs ad castra pervēnērunt. Eās Caesar dūxerat.

Lesson 6, p. 336. A reflexive pronoun always refers to the subject. In English the reflexive pronouns add the ending *self* or *selves* to the objective or possessive (never to the nominative) case of the pronoun.

You hurt yourself by disobeying God.
Christ offered Himself for the sins of man.
We pray for ourselves.

Pupils easily recognize reflexive pronouns of this type. In Latin, however, there are two pronouns of the third person—*is, ea, id* and *suī.* Compare these sentences:

Dux eum laudāvit.
Dux sē laudāvit.

Scīvitne dux ubi mīlitēs ējus essent?
Scīvitne dux ubi mīlitēs suī essent?

Be sure that every pupil in the class can distinguish between a personal pronoun of the third person and a reflexive pronoun of the third person. The reflexive pronoun was introduced in first year (Lesson 11), but not the adjective. Before taking Exercise 37 call attention to the fact that possessive adjectives can be used substantively (equivalent to a noun) as illustrated in the drawing at the bottom of page 338 ("I carry all my possessions with me"). Translate such sentences as:

Caesar suōs laudāvit.
Lēgātus suīs signum dat.
Puer sua omnia sēcum portat.

After pupils understand direct reflexives in simple sentences proceed to complex sentences. Let them first distinguish between reflexive pronouns and non-reflexives; then between direct and indirect reflexives. (These should probably be confined to indirect questions since this is the only construction introduced so far in second year. With a good class, however, it should be possible to use purpose clauses also.)

Caesar rogāvit num mīlitēs sē dēfenderent. (Two translations)
Caesar rogāvit num mīlitēs eum dēfenderent.
Caesar knew where his (own) soldiers had pitched camp.
Caesar knew where their soldiers had pitched camp.

Some of the following may be used to check the students' knowledge of direct and indirect reflexives.

They asked whether Caesar had led out all the hostages with *him*.
Caesar asked whether they had taken all their baggage with *them*.
Christians ask whether Christ will give *them* great rewards.
Christians ask whether Christ will give *His* Mother a great reward.

Exercises 37-40 are classified; Exercise 41 is, as it claims to be, a comprehensive drill on pronouns. Included are personal pronouns, possessive adjectives, and reflexive pronouns and adjectives. The following chart is useful if students have difficulty in translating pronouns and possessive adjectives.

Type (pronoun, adjective, or reflexive)   ....
Person and number   ....
Use in sentence   ....
Case required   ....
Latin form   ....

Lesson 7, p. 344. Grammar assignments refer to: 243-266, 322-324, 330, indicative passive of the four regular conjugations and of *-iō* verbs of the third.

The exact meaning of a passage in Latin is frequently lost because students fail to distinguish clearly and quickly between the active and the passive voice. This fact should be emphasized when the passive forms are taught.

In explaining the distinction in meaning between *ex, dē,* and *ab* it may be helpful to refer to the presentation of these prepositions in Unit Nine of First Year Latin (pages 336-337) and to show students the examples and illustrations given there. Insist on accurate translation into English; do not permit students to say merely "from" when a more specific expression is required.

The third section of Exercise 42 provides a review of the ablative of agent and also of the ablative of means.

Lesson 8, p. 348. Grammar assignments refer to: 128, 133-135, declension of *hic, is, ille;* 464, position of demonstrative adjectives; 479, agreement of pronouns; 790-797, uses of demonstrative pronouns and adjectives.

This lesson presents no special difficulties, with the possible exception of the rule for the use of *hic* and *ille* in contrast (Gr. 795). Some additional sentences may be desired for further drill:

Caesar praised this lieutenant; he did not praise that one.
Caesar hunc lēgātum laudāvit; illum nōn laudāvit.
The soldier and the messenger saw the enemy; the former hastened into the battle and the latter sent a message to Caesar.
Mīles et nuntius hostēs vīdērunt; ille in proelium contendit, hic Caesarī nuntium mīsit.
We shall defend this city, but the enemy will seize that one.
Hanc urbem dēfendēmus, sed hostēs illam occupābunt.
The soldier warned the lieutenant and Caesar. The former feared the enemy, but the latter did not fear them.
Mīles lēgātum et Caesarem monuit. Ille hostēs timēbat, sed hic eōs nōn timēbat.

Both the leaders and the centurions were praised by the commander in chief. The former led all their forces into the territory of the barbarians; the latter fought with their soldiers in the battle line.

Et ducēs et centuriōnēs ā imperātōre laudābantur. Illī omnēs cōpiās suās in fīnēs barbarōrum dūxērunt; hī cum mīlitibus suīs in aciē pugnāvērunt.

Lesson 9, p. 353. Grammar assignments refer to: 267-282, subjunctive passive of the four regular conjugations; 325-326, 330, subjunctive passive of *-iō* verbs of the third conjugation; 546-547, purpose clauses.

Although purpose clauses were studied in Unit Six of FIRST YEAR LATIN and should be familiar to students, experience has shown that it is better to consider them as practically new material. A discussion of purpose clauses may be found on pages 50-52 of this manual. It may be helpful to refer to this material, especially to the six points listed on page 51, when introducing purpose clauses in second year.

Lesson 9, p. 355. Exercise 55 provides an excellent opportunity to stress the necessity of careful and accurate translation from Latin into English. This exercise, using the same verb in various constructions requiring the subjunctive, would be most effective if it were done orally in the classroom, especially if students are alert and call attention to errors on the part of their classmates. Review also primary sequence and secondary sequence.

Lesson 10, p. 357. Grammar assignments refer to: 79-82, third-declension adjectives of three endings and of one ending; 739-740, dative after intransitive verbs.

The manner of listing adjectives of one ending in the vocabulary (LATIN GRAMMAR, page 17, note 1) eliminates any possibility of students construing the second form as a neuter form.

The fact that certain verbs take sole objects in the dative case must be learned when the word is studied in the vocabulary. When these words, or other words governing special cases, occur on the vocabulary charts, students should be given an extra point for adding this information.

Lesson 10, p. 360. Grammar assignments refer to: 331-332, 741, use of impersonal verbs in the passive. This construction requires considerable practice and drill if it is to be mastered. A supple-

mentary exercise, which may be assigned if time permits, is given
below. Both active and passive forms are included. Note that
the verb in sentence 4 *(resistō)* does not have an object in the
dative case.

1. The enemy were resisted by Caesar's legions. 2. The soldier
was not harmed by the lieutenant. 3. Caesar was in command of
the Roman legions in Gaul. 4. The cavalry remained behind to
defend the camp. 5. Roman soldiers were devoted to the glory of
Rome. 6. The daring forces of the enemy were not being resisted
by the legion. 7. Caesar's soldiers were striving after the rewards
of victory. 8. The leader put his lieutenant in command of the
horsemen. 9. Our soldiers will resist the attack and overcome the
enemy. 10. The lieutenant was put in command of the legions by
the general.

1. Hostibus ā legiōnibus Caesaris resistēbātur. 2. Mīlitī ā lēgātō
nōn nocēbātur. 3. Caesar legiōnibus Rōmānīs in Galliā praeerat.
4. Equitēs restitērunt ut castra dēfenderent. 5. Mīlitēs Rōmānī
Rōmae glōriae studuērunt. 6. Cōpiīs audācibus hostium ā legiōne
nōn resistēbātur. 7. Mīlitēs Caesaris victōriae praemiīs studēbant.
8. Dux lēgātum suum equitibus praefēcit. 9. Mīlitēs nostrī im-
petuī resistent et hostēs superābunt. 10. Lēgātus ā imperātōre
legiōnibus praefectus est.

Lesson 11, p. 363. Grammar assignments refer to: 334-335, indicative and subjunctive of deponent verbs; 561, *cum*-temporal
clauses in past time.

The actual conjugation of deponent verbs should not cause
difficulty. However, since students have not yet studied the present passive infinitive, it might be well to refer to page 421 before
introducing deponent verbs. Call attention to the fact that the
passive infinitive of the first, second, and fourth conjugations is
formed by changing the final *e* of the present active infinitive to *ī ;*
in the third conjugation *ī* is the entire passive ending for both
regular verbs and *-iō* verbs. Without this information, it would
not be easy for students to recognize third-conjugation deponents.

The principal parts of deponent verbs are found in Gr. 334. Let
students write the conjugation of these verbs in the indicative and

subjunctive mood on the board or in notebooks. See the exercise on recognition of the forms of deponent verbs in LATIN PROGRESS TESTS, SECOND YEAR, page 43.

The *cum*-temporal clause in past time is a construction that seldom causes trouble, even for slower students.

Lesson 12, p. 369. Grammar assignments refer to: 89-98, comparison of adjectives; 101-102, declension of comparatives and superlatives; 777-780, ablative of comparison; 853-854, 856-857, translation of comparative and superlative adjectives.

Note that, with the exception of those adjectives that use the adverbs *magis* and *maximē,* the comparative degree has the endings of the third declension in all genders; the superlative degree has the endings of the first and second declensions. (In connection with adjectives like *dubius* and *idōneus* it might be well to call attention to the awkward forms that would result if they were to follow the regular rules.) Only the six adjectives of the third declension ending in *-lis* mentioned in GR. 96 add *-limus* to the stem to form the superlative. All others (*ūtilis, nōbilis,* and so forth) follow the regular rule and add *-issimus.*

Another point to which attention should be called is that when the comparative forms are written as they appear at the top of page 368 (for example, *fortior, fortius*) the first form is both masculine and feminine nominative; the second form is neuter nominative (like *gravis, e*). In the declension of comparatives stress must be placed on those cases which are underlined in GR. 101. (The stem is found from the genitive masculine singular; the endings in the ablative singular, genitive plural, and neuter nominative and accusative plural are like *lēx* and *flūmen,* not like *pars* or *gravis.*)

The table on page 75 could be reproduced on the board to help students get an overall picture of the comparative and superlative degrees of adjectives of various types.

Lesson 12, p. 370. Use of *quam* with adjectives in the comparative degree (Exercise 72) should present no difficulties as long as students remember that it takes the same case after as before it. Point out that the ablative of comparison (Exercise 73) is used

COMPARISON OF ADJECTIVES

	POSITIVE			COMPARATIVE[1]			SUPERLATIVE		
	Masc.	*Fem.*	*Neut.*	*Masc.*	*Fem.*	*Neut.*	*Masc., Fem., Neut.*		
Adjectives of the first and second declensions	alt-us	alt-a	alt-um	alt-ior	alt-ior	alt-ius	alt-issimus, a, um		
	integer	integr-a	integr-um	integr-ior	integr-ior	integr-ius	integer-rimus, a, um		
	miser	miser-a	miser-um	miser-ior	miser-ior	miser-ius	miser-rimus, a, um		
	dubi-us	dubi-a	dubi-um	magis dubi-us	magis dubi-a	magis dubi-um	maximē dubi-us, a, um		
Adjectives of the third declension	brev-is	brev-is	brev-e	brev-ior	brev-ior	brev-ius	brev-issimus, a, um		
	ācer	ācr-is	ācr-e	ācr-ior	ācr-ior	ācr-ius	ācer-rimus, a, um		
	diligēns	diligēns	diligēns	diligent-ior	diligent-ior	diligent-ius	diligent-issimus, a, um		
	facil-is	facil-is	facil-e	facil-ior	facil-ior	facil-ius	facil-limus, a, um		

[1] All adjectives have the third-declension endings in the comparative degree with the exception of those which form the comparative by using *magis*.

only when *quam* would be followed by the nominative or accusative case, and that it is never used when any confusion or ambiguity might result.

Lesson 13, p. 375. Grammar assignments refer to: 139, declension of the relative pronoun; 479, agreement of pronouns with their antecedents; 615-618, syntax of relative clauses with the indicative; 625 (546), relative clauses expressing purpose.

The relative pronoun and relative clauses were taught in Unit Six of FIRST YEAR LATIN and should be familiar to almost all students. Suggestions for presenting the material on relative clauses may be found on pages 53-55 of this manual. The explanation of relative clauses with the indicative on pages 246-47 of FIRST YEAR LATIN should also prove helpful. It is possible that the correct English translation of the relative pronoun (especially with regard to the use of *who* and *whom*) may present a problem to those students who do not have a fundamental knowledge of English grammar.

The following sentences illustrate the rule that the case of the relative pronoun depends on its use in its own clause; the gender and number agree with the antecedent of the pronoun.

Nom. Mary, *who* is our mother, loves all men.
      Marīa, *quae* māter nostra est, hominēs omnēs dīligit.
Gen. Mary, *whose* children we are, will pray for us.
      Marīa, *cūjus* līberī sumus, prō nōbīs ōrābit.
Dat. Mary, to *whom* the angel Gabriel gave a message, is Christ's mother.
      Marīa, *cui* angelus Gabriēl nuntium dedit, māter Chrīstī est.
Acc. Mary, *whom* we shall see in heaven, prays for all men.
      Marīa, *quam* in Caelō vidēbimus, prō omnibus hominibus ōrat.
      Mary is the woman Christ called Mother. (The relative pronoun *whom* is understood in English, but must be expressed in Latin.)
      Marīa est mulier *quam* Chrīstus Mātrem appellāvit.
Abl. Mary, in *whom* are all virtues, will help us.
      Marīa, in *quā* omnēs virtūtēs sunt, nōs adjuvābit.

Few students have much difficulty in determining when a relative pronoun should be used to introduce a purpose clause. The important rules to remember are as follows:

1. When the object of the main verb is the subject of the subordinate purpose clause, a relative pronoun is ordinarily used

instead of *ut* to introduce the purpose clause. (The Germans sent infantry to [who would] fight against the French.)

2. A relative pronoun cannot be used to introduce the purpose clause when the relative pronoun would have to agree with the *subject* of an *active main verb*. (He came to see Rome.)

3. When the purpose clause is negative *nē* must be used.

Lesson 13, p. 378. The readings on this page and on pages 384, 389, and 393 furnish valuable background for the account of Caesar's conquests in Gaul, which the students will begin to read in Lesson 17.

Lesson 14, p. 380. Grammar assignments refer to: 99, irregular comparatives and superlatives; 851, syntax of certain adjectives.

Experience has shown that students in general are quite weak on adjectives which have irregular comparative and superlative forms. GRAMMAR 99, 1-6, should therefore be stressed and thorough study of these adjectives should be insisted upon.

Lesson 14, p. 382. The most important point to emphasize concerning these phrases indicating place is that such words as *top, bottom, middle,* and so forth, are adjectives in Latin, and must agree with their nouns in case. They are *not* followed by the genitive as would seem to be required by the English. Use the ablative to express place where or from which; the accusative to express place to which (GR. 915-917).

Lesson 14, p. 383. In the singular *plūs* is always a noun and is followed by the genitive case (literally, *more of*). In the plural it is an adjective; that is, it is put into the same case as the plural noun which it modifies. Like other adjectives both *plūs* and *plūrēs* may be used as nouns (GR. 845-848 and sentences 2, 5 in Exercise 86, B and 1 in Exercise 87). Do not omit Exercise 86; this exercise provides the drill which students need on the use of *plūs* and *plūrēs*.

Lesson 15, p. 387. Grammar assignments refer to: 362-365, 375-376, conjugation of *eō*; 761, accusative of extent of space and time.

Lesson 15, p. 388. Exercises 91 and 92 provide an excellent review of various uses of the subjunctive, as well as of *eō* and its compounds. Call attention to the fact that *eō* and its compounds have two perfect stems, both of which occur in the exercises.

Lesson 16, p. 390. Grammar assignments refer to: 103-111, formation and comparison of adverbs; 686, 690, partitive genitive with *satis* and other adverbs used as nouns.

Lesson 16, p. 391. Exercise 94 provides a review of the comparison of adjectives and drill on the comparison of adverbs. The adverbs in the vocabulary are examples of those that are not formed regularly. *Satis* is another undeclinable noun used with the genitive (like *plūs*).

Lesson 17, p. 396. Grammar assignments refer to: 84-87, irregular adjectives; 114-116, declension of numerals; 766-767, ablative of separation; 770, ablative of respect; 822-828, one . . . other (another).

The grammar introduced in this lesson is not difficult, but the number of assignments included makes it necessary to cover the material slowly. Do not omit any of the exercises, for students will need all the drill that is provided. The words used for *one*, *one . . . other (another)*, and the *other* (GR. 822-828) should be thoroughly explained and discussed in class.

The study of Caesar begins with this lesson. The first two lines of "The Helvetian Drive to the West" may be assigned after students have studied the declension of *ūnus*, *trēs*, and *alius*. The teacher should make sure that all students have read the background material in Part I of the textbook, pages 3-7, and also the introduction to Part II on pages 17-18. Students who are taking a course in world history may enlarge on some of the topics if there is sufficient time. The comparison on pages 12-13 makes an effective summary when all the books have been covered.

Lesson 18, pp. 406, 409, 412. Grammar assignments refer to: 362, 369-371, 386-387, conjugation of *ferō*; 907-909, 911, participles; 138, declension of *ipse*; 808-810, 812, the intensive pronoun and adjective.

Students have no choice but to memorize (and they usually remember) the principal parts of *ferō*. The present indicative active (the passive of the present system is not assigned) must also be memorized. The imperfect and future tenses follow the rules for regular third-conjugation verbs on the stem *fer-*. All the perfect tenses are formed regularly. If the student uses the easy rule for the imperfect subjunctive, present infinitive + personal endings, he will have no difficulty with this tense.

The Latin participle is used very frequently. For this reason an understanding of the participial phrase in both Latin and English is extremely important. The student should be taught to grasp the participial phrase as a *thought phrase* to be definitely associated with the word with which the participle agrees. In Latin the participle is usually placed at the end of the participial phrase. Adverbial modifiers regularly precede the participle.

Exercise 110 could well be used as an oral drill. If some students are slow in giving the perfect participles, stress once more the need for learning the principal parts of all verbs as they occur in the vocabularies of the lessons. Exercise 111 is also a good one to take orally during the class period.

Ipse can be used either as an adjective (GR. 808) or as a pronoun (GR. 812). Note that it is used as an adjective in all the sentences of Exercise 115 and as a pronoun in sentences 2, 3, and 5 of Exercise 116. (*Ipse* means *self,* but is rarely used in the first or second persons in Latin.)

In English the compound personal pronouns (myself, ourselves; yourself, yourselves; himself, herself, itself, themselves) are used both as intensive pronouns (God Himself gave us a free will) and as reflexive pronouns (Christ offered Himself for the sins of man). Latin, however, has *ipse* for the intensive and *sui* (always in the oblique cases) as the reflexive pronoun. One way of distinguishing between intensive and reflexive pronouns in simple sentences is that the intensive pronouns may be omitted without substantially changing the meaning of a sentence. (The king himself came; The king came.) If a reflexive pronoun is omitted, there is no sentence.

---

[1] There are only a few instances in which students might maintain that a reflexive pronoun could be omitted and a complete and unambiguous statement remain. See, for example "All Gaul in Arms," line 48, page 175: *Ubi Haedui discessērunt, Biturīgēs statim sē cum Avernīs jungunt.*

(The king praised himself; The king praised . . .)[1] A reflexive
pronoun always refers to the subject of the sentence, or to the
subject of the principal or subordinate clause in a compound sentence (page 337). The intensive pronoun may emphasize the subject or any other word in the sentence. (We are made to the image
of God Himself.)

Lesson 18, p. 414. Deponent verbs are very useful because they
enable us to translate an English perfect participle active into
Latin in such sentences as: Having set out for the city, Caesar
arrived on the third day. The translation of such participles is
discussed in great detail on pages 448-449, after the student has
studied the ablative absolute.

Lesson 19, pp. 420, 422. Grammar assignments refer to: 398-
401, 411-413, conjugation of the irregular verb *possum;* 888-896,
uses of the infinitive.

Footnote 1 on page 80 of LATIN GRAMMAR is important, for if
students apply these rules, they will not have to rely on a mechan-
ical memorization of the conjugation of *possum*. One effective way
of teaching this verb is to write *pos sum* on the chalk board, explaining that this verb is a compound of *pos* (sometimes *pot*)
and *sum*. Then ask a student to write the present tense of *sum*, or
write it as the student recites the forms; put the prefix *pos* before
each form that begins with *s* and *pot* before each form that begins
with *e*. Students can write the imperfect and future indicative and
the present subjunctive without further instructions. The principal parts should now be studied. Note that the imperfect subjunctive follows the rule of present infinitive + personal ending
(the GRAMMAR must be consulted for macrons). The perfect
tenses are formed regularly.

Possum is not an independent verb; it requires a present infinitive to complete its meaning. (See the notation "w. pres. infin."
in vocabulary.) With transitive verbs this infinitive may be active
or passive. Students are familiar with the present infinitive from
the principal parts of regular, irregular, and deponent verbs. Give
students as much practice as may be necessary in translating
Latin and English phrases like the samples on page 81.

Vocāre potestis.   We can pray.
Cōnārī potest.   You can hear.
Jacere possunt.   He can see.
Venīre poterimus.   We were able to flee.
Pugnāre poterant.   He could ask.

Note that when the infinitive is used as subject or predicate noun, it may also be translated by an English noun or gerund (verbal noun). *Bonum est ōrāre: To pray* is good; *Prayer* is good; *Praying* is good.

Lesson 19, p. 428. This idiomatic use of *quam* (with a superlative adjective or adverb) is easily forgotten and will probably have to be taught more than once. Two examples occur in the Latin reading assigned for this lesson, one in line 27 and the other in line 68. It will help the class to remember the construction if someone is called on to explain the idiom when these sentences are translated.

Lesson 20, pp. 434-438, 440. Grammar assignments refer to: 885-887, tense by relation; 897-899, accusative with the infinitive; 800-804, reflexive pronouns; 473-474, 900, predicate nouns and adjectives in the accusative with the infinitive; 331, impersonal verbs in the accusative with the infinitive.

Because the accusative with the infinitive is a construction that occurs frequently in Caesar, it must be thoroughly understood and recognized with ease. With slow students it may be necessary to analyze each sentence in Exercise 132 in some such manner as the following:

Are there any verbs in the first sentence? *(Dīcō, pugnāre)* What kind of verb is *dīcō?* (Verb of saying) What construction is very common after a verb of saying? (Accusative with the infinitive)[1] Is there an infinitive in this sentence? *(pugnāre)* What does it mean? (to fight) Are there any nouns in the accusative case? *(mīlitēs;* soldiers) Could *soldiers* be the subject of *fight?* (Yes, soldiers fight.) Translate the entire sentence. (I say that all our soldiers fight [are fighting] bravely.)

---

[1] If a pupil should reply that indirect questions follow verbs of *saying,* ask for the interrogative word and the subjunctive. Since there is neither in this sentence, an indirect question must be ruled out.

In Exercise 133 the analysis would proceed as follows: Point out the verbs in the first sentence. (know; are) What kind of sentence is this? (Complex) What is the main clause? (I know) What is the subordinate clause? (that there are ten cohorts in one legion) What construction usually follows a verb of knowing? (Accusative with the infinitive) What is the verb in the subordinate clause that will be translated as an infinitive? (are; *esse*) What is the subject of *are?* (cohorts) What case will be used for cohorts and why? (Accusative because it is the subject of an infinitive) Is the English conjunction *that* translated in Latin? (No, it is an introductory word that is not translated in Latin) What part of speech is *ten?* (Adjective modifying *cohorts*) How do you translate the phrase *in one legion? (in ūnā legiōne)* Translate the sentence. *(Sciō decem cohortēs in ūnā legiōne esse.)*

When the perfect and future infinitives have been taught, some additional questions will have to be included: What is the tense of the main verb? Does the action of the verb in the subordinate clause take place before, at the same time as, or after the action of the verb in the main clause? What tense of the infinitive will be required in Latin? (If the tense of the infinitive to be used is a compound tense containing a participle, further questions will be required: What is the gender and number of the subject? What form of the participle agrees with this subject?)

Certain points will require special drill and emphasis; particularly, when the English word *that* follows a verb of *knowing, saying, asking,* and the like, it is not translated in Latin (compare with *there, it*);[1] a present infinitive is used whenever the action expressed by the verb in the subordinate clause takes place at the same time as the action expressed by the main verb (that action may be present, past, or future); in compound tenses of the infinitive the participle must agree in gender and number with the accusative subject of the infinitive.

---

[1] Do not permit students to think the word *that* is *never* translated. The demonstrative adjective, the relative pronoun, and the word introducing a purpose or result clause must be translated.

Some of the more intelligent members of the class may notice that the indirect question may also follow verbs of *saying* and *knowing* (as well as *asking*). If no one in the class brings up the subject, it would be best to make no reference to the indirect question, for the discussion might be confusing to students who do not thoroughly understand both constructions. If the problem of distinguishing between the two does come up, it may be pointed out that the indirect question in English has an interrogative word *(why, where, who, what)* or at least *whether*. In Latin the indirect question has an interrogative pronoun, adjective, or adverb *(num* or *-ne* for *whether)* and the verb is in the subjunctive, not the infinitive.

Lesson 20, p. 437. It may be helpful at this time to summarize the various tenses of the infinitive. All forms of the infinitive have now been taught except the future passive, which is not included in second year.

REGULAR VERBS

	PRESENT	PERFECT	FUTURE
Active	to call voc-āre (-ēre, -ere, īre)	to have called vocāv-isse	to be about to call vocāt-ūrus (a, um) esse
Passive	to be called voc-ārī (-ērī, -ī, -īrī)	to have been called vocātus (a, um) esse	

DEPONENT VERBS

	PRESENT	PERFECT	FUTURE
Active	to try cōn-ārī (-ērī, -ī, -īrī)	to have tried cōnātus (a, um) esse	to be about to try cōnāt-ūrus (a, um) esse

Lesson 20, p. 439. Exercises 140 and 141 direct the students' attention to the use of the reflexive pronoun in the accusative with infinitive construction. Sentences 1 and 2 of Exercise 140 show very clearly the difference in meaning between *suī* and *is* when used as the subject of the subordinate clause in this construction.

Lesson 20, p. 441. The teacher must stress sentence 5 in Exercise 144 so that students will not have trouble with sentences 4 and 7 in Exercise 145. Since *oportet* can be followed only by the present infinitive (as noted in the vocabulary), past time (I say that Pilate should have saved the life of Christ) is expressed by using the perfect infinitive of *oportet*. Sentence 4 in Exercise 145 should be translated: *Putāsne nōn oportuisse Caesarem Gallīs nocēre?* Sentence 7: *Putāsne oportuisse Caesarem cum Gallīs bellum gerere?*

Lesson 20, p. 442. Because this lesson introduces a large amount of new material, it should be followed by a thorough review. It would be best to assign Exercise 146 as written work so that each student's paper can be carefully graded and checked. Points in which a number of students are weak can then be gone over a second time and any difficulties cleared up.

Lesson 21, pp. 446, 448, 450. Grammar assignments refer to: 886, perfect infinitives and perfect participles in tense by relation; 912-914, ablative absolute; 141, declension of interrogative adjective; 502-503, direct questions; 660-662, indirect questions.

There must be at least two words in the ablative case in order to have an ablative absolute: (1) a noun or pronoun and (2) a participle, adjective, or noun in agreement with it. Since this construction involves a participle, either expressed or understood,[1] there will necessarily be a relationship of time between the action expressed by the ablative absolute and the action expressed by the main verb. The perfect participle passive, indicating that the action expressed in the ablative absolute took place before the action of the main verb, is used most frequently.

Note that Exercise 147 requires that the ablative absolute be translated by a temporal clause in English. Such translations should be called for whenever possible, for a literal translation results in stilted English. Several good English translations of the various kinds of ablative absolute are suggested in GR. 913.

Lesson 21, pp. 448-449. The notes on these pages require thorough study so that students will be able to translate English sentences containing active past participles.

[1] When no Latin participle is expressed some form of *sum*, which has only a future participle in Latin, must be supplied in the English translation.

Lesson 21, p. 450. This section on the use of the interrogative adjective presents an excellent opportunity to review direct and indirect questions. The Latin review questions in Exercise 155 contain many examples of the interrogative adjective.

Lesson 22, p. 456. Grammar assignments refer to: 82, 307, declension of the present participle; 885, tense by relation; 907-911, use of participles.

The present participle is declined like *dīligēns* (third declension) except in the ablative singular (GR. 307). The translation of present participles should be stressed in Exercises 160 and 161. Sometimes students get the mistaken notion that the ablative absolute can be used only with passive participles. The section on the use of the present participle, an active form, in the ablative absolute should therefore receive special attention. Note the position of the ablative absolute in Latin sentences, usually at the beginning of the sentence.

Lesson 22, p. 460. Exercise 167 provides a review of many constructions: direct question, indirect question, purpose clause, hortative subjunctive, ablative of manner, accusative with infinitive, reflexive pronoun, temporal clause in past time, adjective governing a special case, ablative of comparison, participle, *hic . . . ille* or *alter . . . alter.* Such review exercises should be used to encourage students by showing them how much they have learned.

Lesson 23, pp. 463, 464. Grammar assignments refer to: 398, 402-404, 414-417, conjugation of *volō;* 556-557, temporal clauses expressing a single past act. The verb *volō* may be followed by an infinitive or the accusative with the infinitive, but it may also be used as any transitive verb. (What do you wish?)

Lesson 23, p. 464. Students may have a certain amount of trouble remembering that the present perfect is used even where the English would seem to require the pluperfect (GR. 557). Note that the perfect indicative is used only to express a *single* past act. Students have also studied *cum*-temporal clauses in past time (Lesson 11) which described the circumstances and required the subjunctive mood.

Exercise 170 will probably seem difficult, for the sentences are quite long and include practice on a number of the more involved constructions which have been taught in previous lessons. It should not be omitted.

The reading assignment for this lesson contains an example of the idiomatic use of *quam* (line 39) and provides an opportunity to review this idiom if students have forgotten it.

Lesson 24, pp. 471, 473. Grammar assignments refer to: 362, 366-368, 381-382, 384, conjugation of *fīō* (passive of *faciō*); 637-640, noun *ut*-clauses.

Lesson 24, p. 472. Noun clauses introduced by *ut* present no special problems. However, the verbs which are usually followed by clauses of this type must be learned (GR. 638-639). Remind students that this information is always given in the lesson vocabularies (see page 470) and should be learned as part of the "equipment" of the word.

Lesson 25, pp. 476, 479. Grammar assignments refer to: 550-551, 554, result clauses; 633-634, 636, characteristic clauses; 919-922, rules for time.

Students will probably have no trouble in identifying result clauses in Latin because the main clause furnishes a clue in the form of the adverb of degree or manner. There will be more difficulty in recognizing result clauses in English, especially when they are relative clauses. It will be helpful to analyze a number of clauses in English and have students decide whether they are purpose clauses, result clauses, characteristic clauses, or simple adjective clauses. A few examples are given below.

The man who conquered Gaul was Caesar. (Adjective clause)

He sent cavalry to fight the enemy. (Purpose clause)

He is not one to say such things. (Result or characteristic clause; it is a result of his particular characteristics as a person that he does not say certain things)

He commanded the soldiers to withdraw. (Noun *ut*-clause)

One legion remained behind to defend the Roman camp. (Purpose clause)

There is no one who does not fear war. (Characteristic clause)

Christ, who came to save us from our sins, loves all men. (Adjective clause and purpose clause)

None are so daring as to attack the column. (Result clause)

He who serves God is a good man. (Adjective clause)

No hardship is so great that it cannot be overcome by a brave man. (Result clause)

Who is there in the camp that does not know these things? (Characteristic clause)

The soldier who led the legion into battle was very brave. (Adjective clause)

The Gauls sent envoys to seek peace. (Purpose clause)

Exercise 182 provides practice in recognizing result and characteristic clauses in Latin. There are characteristic clauses in sentences 4, 8, 9, 10, 11, 12, 13, and 14. Sentences 1, 2, 5, 6, 7, and 15 contain result clauses which can be easily identified from the adverb of degree or manner in the main clause. Sentence 3 could be considered either a result clause or a purpose clause.

The sentences in Exercise 183 could be analyzed in class before they are assigned for translation. All except sentences 3, 4, and 10 contain result clauses introduced by *ut*. Sentences 3 and 4 contain characteristic clauses. There is a relative result clause introduced by *quī* in sentence 10. Exercise 187 provides further practice in translating result clauses.

If students have trouble in determining from the English whether an adverb of degree *(tam, adeō)* or an adverb of manner *(sīc, ita)* is required in a given instance, explain that adverbs of degree usually modify adverbs and adjectives (so carefully, so bravely, so high, so difficult) and that adverbs of manner modify verbs (he so worked, the saints so lived).

Lesson 25, p. 479. Note that *diēs* is used as a feminine noun in sentence 5 of Exercise 185 (Gr. 70).

Lesson 26, p. 485. Grammar assignments refer to: 212, 228-230, 319, 342, 380, 391, 418, gerunds of verbs of the several conjugations and of irregular verbs; 864, uses of the gerund.

Students often enter Latin classes with very little knowledge of the English gerund or ability to recognize a gerund. It is advisable to spend considerable time on the gerund and make sure that its uses are thoroughly understood before going on to the gerundive in Lessons 27 and 28. Certain points will require special emphasis:

1. The gerund is a verbal noun.[1]
2. It has no nominative case.
3. It is singular number only.
4. It may take objects and be modified by adverbs.
5. It is always active in form and in meaning.

The more common uses of the gerund are indicated in GR. 864. Probably the most frequent use of all is in the accusative case after *ad* to express purpose. This construction is explained more fully in Lesson 28, page 501. Two gerunds, both in the accusative case after *ad,* occur in the reading assignment for this lesson (lines 38 and 46). Line 35 contains a gerundive. Since this form is not studied until the following lesson, the word is explained in a footnote. It is wise to make a careful analysis of all the italicized words (not all of which are gerunds) in Exercise 190.

Lesson 27, pp. 491-499. Grammar assignments refer to: 288, 304-306, 329, 344, 385, 396, the gerundive of regular and irregular verbs; 865, 868, 878-883, uses of the gerundive.

Three points of distinction between gerunds and gerundives are to be emphasized:

1. The gerund is a noun; the gerundive is an adjective.

---

[1] Students studying English grammar are required to distinguish between gerunds, participles, and progressive verb forms, all of which are verb forms ending in *ing*. The Latin teacher may also find it necessary to test students on such forms as:

They gained the victory by *fighting* bravely. (Gerund, a verbal noun)

Fighting bravely, the soldiers sustained the attack and defeated the enemy. (Participle, a verbal adjective)

The first legion was *fighting* on the hill. (Progressive verb form)

Some nouns also end in *ing:*

Men waited for the *coming* of Christ.

We heard the *shouting* of the enemy.

2. The gerund is active in meaning; the gerundive is passive.

3. The gerund has four cases and is always singular in number; the gerundive has all cases, may be singular or plural, and must agree in number and gender with the noun it modifies.

The gerundive has no English equivalent; hence its special uses will have to be covered slowly. Note that Exercises 197-204 are classified and that each group of Latin sentences is followed by a group of English sentences involving the same construction. Literal translations are necessary when the construction is explained to pupils. Insist, however, on good English translations of the Latin sentences.

After the completion of Exercises 197-202, covering the use of the gerundive with *sum* (Gr. 878-882),[1] the following instructions may be given to students:

1. Watch the verb; the gerundive is always passive.

   a. If the verb in the English sentence is passive, the gerundive must agree with the subject.

     The soldiers should be warned.

     Mīlitēs monendī sunt. (Masculine plural)

   b. If the verb is active and has an accusative object, change to the passive and translate:

     We should praise this man. (This man should be praised by us.)

     Hic vir nōbīs laudandus est.

   c. If the verb has no object or is intransitive, change to the impersonal passive.

     We must conquer. (It must be conquered.)

     Vincendum est. (Neuter ending)

   d. If the verb takes any case other than the accusative, change to the impersonal passive and put the object (of an active verb) or subject (of a passive verb) in the case governed by the verb.

     We must resist enemies. (It must be resisted to enemies.)

---

[1] Do not confuse students by referring to the gerundive with *sum* as the passive periphrastic conjugation. This term is not used in the Henle Latin Series.

Enemies must be resisted. (It must be resisted to enemies.)

Hostibus resistendum est. (Neuter ending)

2. Watch the agent; the subject of an active verb becomes the agent when the verb is changed to passive form.

    a. Put the agent in the dative case unless there is another dative in the clause.

       Men should love God. (God should be loved by men.)

       Deus hominibus dīligendus est. (Masculine ending)

    b. If there is another dative in the clause, use *ab (ā)* and the ablative to express the agent.

       Men should serve God. (It should be served to God by men.)

       Deō ab hominibus serviendum est. (Neuter ending because *serviō* governs dative case)

Lesson 28, p. 500. Grammar assignments refer to: 865-872, uses of the gerundive.

This lesson is devoted to a study of the gerundive as an attributive adjective. As stated previously, the gerundive has no English equivalent, but when the gerund would have an accusative object, Latin uses the gerundive construction (noun and attributive adjective) instead of the gerund. Compare these English sentences:

They captured the territory by fighting fiercely.

They captured the territory by defeating the Gauls.

The first sentence is similar to those found in Exercise 191 of the lesson on gerunds. The gerund is modified by the adverb *fiercely* and is used as an ablative of means.

Fīnēs ācriter pugnandō cēpērunt.

In the second sentence the gerund has an object in the accusative case. Latin prefers the gerundive construction in such cases (GR. 870) because the gerund would have two nouns in the accusative case *(Fīnēs Gallōs vincendō cēpērunt).* In changing to the gerundive, put the accusative object of the gerund (Gauls) in the case of the gerund (ablative of means). The gerundive is then made to agree with the noun it modifies *(vincendīs)* and the preferred translation is:

Fīnēs Gallīs vincendīs cēpērunt.

Compare the two sentences as often as necessary. Stress these rules: If there is no accusative object, use the gerund; if the gerund would have an accusative object, use the gerundive. Put the noun in the case that would be required if one were using a gerund and make the gerundive agree with the noun. These are also applicable in the case of gerunds and gerundives to express purpose on pages 501-502.

For those pupils who have difficulty in determining whether a given form in a Latin sentence is a gerund or a gerundive, suggest the following tests: If the Latin word is in the nominative case, has a feminine ending, or is plural, it must be a gerundive. If there is a noun in the same case as the verb form, it must be a gerundive. This gerundive is a passive verbal adjective; translate literally first, then change into a good English translation. For example, *urbis videndae* = of the city to be seen; a better English translation is: of seeing the city. The gerund is active and is translated by the English gerund.

The reading from Caesar to be assigned with this lesson does not contain any gerunds, but there are six gerundives. Students should be called on to identify these as they occur and to tell why a gerundive construction is used instead of a gerund. In each case (lines 122, 131, 140, 159, 168, and 169) the gerund should not be used because it would take an accusative object.

Lesson 29, pp. 505, 508. Grammar assignments refer to: 28, formation of the vocative; 463, 678, position and use of the vocative; 208, 216-218, 283, 289-291, 317, 327, 377, 383, 388, 394, 421, formation of the imperative; 515-517, commands in the second person; 1020, irregular imperatives.

The vocative case should present no difficulties. It is exactly like the nominative, singular or plural, except for certain nouns of the second declension in the singular (GR. 28).

Beginning with this lesson the grammar assignments are quite light and there are no formal reading assignments given in the textbook. It is hoped that these short and comparatively simple lessons will give the teacher an opportunity to assign more extensive reading, especially from "All Gaul in Arms" and the selections from Christian Latin.

The teacher may also wish at this time to begin a review of the year's work. The classified review exercises in the textbook (pages 526-543) are designed to cover the major constructions studied in second year and provide sufficient material for quite a thorough review.

Lesson 29, p. 507. Special attention should be given to the formation of the plural imperative of third-conjugation verbs. Both regular verbs and *-iō* verbs of the third conjugation have *e* in the singular, but *i* in the plural: mitt-e, mitt-*i*te; cap-e, cap-*i*te. This is also true of the passive imperative of third-conjugation verbs: mitt-ere, mitt-*i*minī; cap-ere, cap-*i*minī.

Lesson 30, p. 514. Grammar assignments refer to: 695-699, genitive of description; 762-763, ablative of description.

The rules governing the particular uses of the genitive of description and the ablative (Gr. 696-698) should be studied carefully. Point out that an adjective must always appear in the descriptive phrase and that no preposition is used with either the genitive or ablative in this construction.

Lesson 31, p. 517. Grammar assignments refer to: 572-573, 578, causal clauses.

Since only the more simple causal clauses are included in this assignment, there should be no special difficulties.

Lesson 32, p. 519. Grammar assignments refer to: 729-730, dative of purpose; 731, double dative.

Although both the dative of purpose and the dative of reference can be used independently, they are usually found together to form what is known as the double dative. The restrictions noted in Gr. 730 should not be overlooked.

VOCABULARY CHARTS

Vocabulary charts should be large enough for the entire class to see. They can be printed or lettered on white paper and mounted on cardboards slightly larger, or they can be printed directly on the cardboard. The vocabulary charts here given are arranged in four columns, fifteen words to a column. The vocabulary is listed in the same order as it appears in the text. The entire basal vocabulary of FIRST YEAR LATIN, with the exception of the easily recognizable proper nouns and the expression *in saecula saeculōrum*, is contained in the first eight charts of sixty words each. Charts 9-15 cover the vocabulary of SECOND YEAR LATIN, including all words which occur after the first six units of first year. The Words to Remember from Caesar which correspond to each lesson will be found in the vocabulary charts following the regular vocabulary for that particular lesson.

The vocabulary charts may be used for drill in various ways. One method is outlined below:

1. Each day a different student begins the drill; e.g., the first student in the first row the first day, the second student in the first row the second day, and so forth.

2. Each student is given *five seconds* to pronounce in Latin and to translate as many words as possible of the vocabulary studied to date.

3. Each succeeding student *continues* where the previous student stopped when the teacher said "Next" or "Time" or a student tapped a bell.

4. The number of points scored (one point for *each* meaning given) is recorded by the student on a 3″ x 5″ file card, kept in his Latin book for this purpose.

5. The entire class is alert to correct mistakes either in pronunciation or meaning. For each error corrected two points are earned. (If a student indicates he wishes to make a correction but instead makes an error himself, he must subtract two points from his score.)

6. From time to time (preferably after each five opportunities) the total is recorded on a record chart and later translated to a per cent on the basis of a relative grade for the distributed scores. (No names are called when these totals are given. The students are previously informed where their names occur in the alphabetical list of the members of the class. Anyone not prompt in giving his score is penalized by a loss of points.)

The advantages of this procedure are as follows:

1. It is an easy method of learning a vocabulary.

2. With a class of forty students, the drill approximately takes only five minutes.

3. Every student gets accustomed to answering in class. He will later not hesitate to volunteer when even the most difficult complex sentences are to be analyzed.

4. The element of emulation makes students alert, trains them to accept criticism, and gives a pleasant tone to the class.

Various other uses may be made of the charts, but *meanings* not *forms* is the primary purpose of the charts.

Vocabulary Chart No. 1

(Lessons 1-2, part of Lesson 3, FIRST YEAR LATIN)

terra	fīlius	propter	lēx
porta	Deus	cum	rēx
nauta	amīcus	post	dux
victōria	et	in (abl.)	lūx
silva	bellum	sum	homō
glōria	caelum	es	imperātor
ōrat	rēgnum	est	vēritās
ōrant	praemium	sumus	salūs
videt	perīculum	estis	vōx
vident	imperium	sunt	audīvit
nōn	dedit	quod	virtūs
laudat	dedērunt	itaque	mīles
laudant	gladius	incolunt	pāx
prōvincia	sed	vidētis	via
servus	oppidum	vīcērunt	populus

Vocabulary Chart No. 2

(Lessons 3-6, part of Lesson 7, FIRST YEAR LATIN)

mūnīvērunt	corpus	in (acc.)	cōpia
pars	vulnus	nunc	cōpiae
collis	agmen	autem	posuērunt castra
hostis	nōmen	fēcērunt	agunt grātiās
gēns	mundus	vēnit	magnus
caedēs	erat	vēnērunt	altus
frāter	erant	rēs	bonus
pater	adventus	fidēs	longus
māter	equitātus	aciēs	malus
mōns	exercitus	spēs	multus
clāmor	impetus	posuērunt	sānctus
prīnceps	metus	castra	prīmus
occīdērunt	spīritus	impedīmenta	angustus
flūmen	portus	grātia	reliquus
iter	senātus	grātiae	tūtus

Vocabulary Chart No. 3

(Lessons 7-10, part of Lesson 11, FIRST YEAR LATIN)

prō	plēnus	pugnō	aliēnus
inopia	fīnitimus	superō	ōrātiō
dominus	similis	portō	semper
mūrus	et . . . et	centuriō	sīcut
frūmentum	quid	numerus	in prīncipiō
legiō	prīmā lūce	dō	-ne
gravis	urbs	vocō	moneō
brevis	pōns	interim	timeō
commūnis	signum	mors	terreō
difficilis	eques	hīberna	habeō
facilis	laudō	ubi	arma
fortis	occupō	quis	ego
nōbilis	oppugnō	quid	nōs
omnis	ōrō	cūr	videō
cupidus	parō	locus	saepe

Vocabulary Chart No. 4

(Lessons 11-15, part of Lesson 16, FIRST YEAR LATIN)

tū	īnstruō	conveniō	incendō
vōs	mittō	per	tum
teneō	fortiter	undique	puer
moveō	vincō	tēlum	ager
tamen	petō	absum	vir
neque	pellō	longē	fortūna
is (personal)	litterae	collocō	ita
sustineō	pōnō	maneō	trāns
fīnēs	contendō	compleō	miser
suī	agō	cēdō	līber
etiam	ibi	atque	integer
enim	dē	incitō	proelium
dūcō	audiō	adjuvō	cīvitās
gerō	mūniō	servō	meus
dēfendō	veniō	perturbō	noster

Vocabulary Chart No. 5

(Lessons 16-23, part of Lesson 24, FIRST YEAR LATIN)

tuus	dīmittō	novus	quī, quae, quod
vester	occīdō	diū	auxilium
administrō	sine	ācriter	auxilia
appellō	ferē	expugnō	memoria
cōnfirmō	vehementer	tribūnus	memoriā teneō
cōnservō	explōrō	cōnsilium	ad
nam	premō	concilium	usque
ab (ā)	retineō	lēgātus	perveniō
contineō	comparō	lātus	pertineō
obtineō	vīta	facile	parātus
aut	vallum	labor (noun)	ūtilis
aut ... aut	amīcitia	ōrdō	nox
neque ... neque	fossa	obses	dēdūcō
posteā	celeriter	inter	cognōscō
trādō	exspectō	statim	nuntius

Vocabulary Chart No. 6

(Lessons 24-28, part of Lesson 29, FIRST YEAR LATIN)

nātūra	plūrimum	genus	adōrō
-que	valeō	aqua	suus
injūria	cernō	cōgō	fuga
diūtius	quis, quid	vērus	dēdō
facilius	ostendō	inquit	rēs pūblica
appropinquō	trādūcō	avē	dīligō
vastō	clam	mora	ante
custōs	socius	doceō	praesidium
ubi	quī (interrog.)	tollō	vērō
cūr	incolō	peccātum	parvus
unde	cōnsistō	regō	mōs
quō	rogō	at	manus
certus	quaerō	mēns	causa
barbarus	quantus	dolor	causā (w. gen.)
apud	mūnītiō	miserēre nōbīs	sciō

Vocabulary Chart No. 7

(Lessons 29-36, part of Lesson 37, FIRST YEAR LATIN)

pācō	cadō	cōnstituō	ūllus
subitō	is (demonstr.)	cōnsuēvī	nūllus
probō	ille	sententia	sōlus
relinquō	numquam	regiō	tōtus
addūcō	praetereā	omnīnō	capiō
commoveō	ratiō	jubeō	fugiō
impediō	līberō	oportet	faciō
auctōritās	vacuus	timor	voluntās
contrā	līber (adj.)	quot	annus
ā tergō	prohibeō	aeternus	vigilia
ā fronte	possum	caput	tempus
summus	adversus (adj.)	alius	diēs
discēdō	proximus	alter	hōra
nāvis	jam	uter	prīmus
ex (ē)	prīmum	neuter	secundus

Vocabulary Chart No. 8

(Lessons 37-42, FIRST YEAR LATIN)

tertius	accipiō	scrībō	orior
conjiciō	cōnficiō	reperiō	polliceor
recipiō	nēmō	negō	loquor
cupiō	magnitūdō	nuntiō	proficīscor
rūrsus	satis (adv.)	dēmōnstrō	nactus
pēs	animus	exīstimō	ēgredior
passus	satis (noun)	sentiō	prōgredior
mīlle	noceō	aestimō	arbitror
mīlia	praesum	jūdicō	hortor
mīlia passuum	mare	quam	eō (verb)
quam (degree)	ventus	certiōrem faciō	exeō
interficiō	nāvigō	cōnor	ineō
ēripiō	dīcō	vereor	trānseō
nihil	respondeō	sequor	redeō
cōnspiciō	putō	patior	adeō (verb)

Vocabulary Chart No. 9

(Lessons 1-6, part of Lesson 7, SECOND YEAR LATIN)

crux	cōnsilium capiō	repellō	meus
classis	faciō	reprimō	noster
cohors	iter faciō	vīvō	tuus
cōnsul	fugiō	praesidium	vester
auctōritās	cupiō	pīlum	is (personal)
lībertās	jaciō	rogō	suī (personal)
timor	-ne	quot	suus
barbarus	num	quantus	recipiō
firmus	nōnne	quō (adv.)	dēdō
plūrimus	quis, quid	sciō	abdō
idōneus	ubi (adv.)	quaerō	dējiciō
proximus	cūr	dolor	cōgō
pācō	redūcō	aperiō	relinquō
incolō	rejiciō	ego	dīvidō
capiō	remittō	tū	fuga

Vocabulary Chart No. 10

(Lessons 7-13, part of Lesson 14, SECOND YEAR LATIN)

in fugam dō	cōnficiō	hortor	apud
ex (ē)	accipiō	vereor	nihil (nīl)
dē	facilius	sequor	nihil (adv.)
ab (ā)	ut	patior	sub (w. abl.)
hic	nē (conj.)	orior	sub (w. acc.)
is (demonstr.)	quō (conj.)	loquor	quī (rel.)
ille	dīligēns	proficīscor	committō
causa	audāx	aggredior	proelium committō
causā (w. gen.)	ācer	cum (conj.)	angustiae
ratiō	celer	cohortor	inquit
dīligō	studeō	prōgredior	peccātum
contrā	resistō	dubius	ante (prep.)
interficiō	praesum	certus	extrēmus
addūcō	noceō	certiōrem faciō	superior
cōnspiciō	praeficiō	quam (adv.)	summus

Vocabulary Chart No. 11

(Lessons 14-18, SECOND YEAR LATIN)

ulterior	passus	alius	referō
ultimus	mīlle passūs	alter	pedem referō
medius	diū	uterque	ipse
eō (verb)	parum (adv.)	duo	praeter
exeō	parum (noun)	trēs	socius
trānseō	satis (adv.)	centum	suscipiō
ineō	satis (noun)	prīmus	vīs
adeō (verb)	tūtō (adv.)	secundus	vī
hōra	multum (adv.)	tertius	indūcō
diēs	facile	prohibeō	mercātor
mīlle	ūllus	lingua	prabtereā
mīlia	nūllus	ferō	quā dē causā
decem	sōlus	īnferō	quoque
quattuor	tōtus	differō	cupiditās
pēs	ūnus	cōnferō	conjūrātiō

Vocabulary Chart No. 12

(Lesson 19, part of Lesson 20, SECOND YEAR LATIN)

possum	quam (w. superl.)	dīcō	intereā
cōnstituō	profectiō	animadvertō	perdūcō
cōnor	lēgātiō	sentiō	castellum
coepī	omnīnō	reperiō	mōs
dēbeō	domō	arbitror	sī
jubeō	fluō	nuntiō	mūnītiō
mandō	rīpa	polliceor	circum
parō	inquiunt	crēdō	hiemō
cōnsequor	putō	dispōnō	quā (rel. adv.)
jungō	negō	cōnscrībō	inde
conjungō	exīstimō	revertor	extrā
permoveō	dēmōnstrō	trādūcō	jam
imperō	cōnfirmō	impediō	paene
oportet	respondeō	concēdō	cōnspectus
parātus	intellegō	spatium	līberī

Vocabulary Chart No. 13

(Lessons 20-22, part of Lesson 23, SECOND YEAR LATIN)

servitūs	jugum	objiciō	ēripiō
explōrātōr	sarcina	conjiciō	vīrēs
quārtus	succēdō	supersum	mājōrēs
vērō	tandem	trīduum	tempus
vigilia	dēfessus	dēditiō	sūmō
nōndum	ēgredior	prōjiciō	tot
amplius	potior	eō (adv.)	ventus
āvertō	vetō	poscō	expellō
fugitīvus	conjūrō	perterreō	hiems
commūtō	commoveō	perfuga	nātiō
convertō	circiter	ut prīmum	regiō
ā novissimō agmine	claudō	cum prīmum	subitus
īnsequor	latus (noun)	postquam	ōceanus
triplex	circumveniō	ubi (conj.)	praefectus
veterānus	anceps	volō	complūrēs

Vocabulary Chart No. 14

(Lessons 23-24, part of Lesson 25, SECOND YEAR LATN)

amplus	suprā	tempestās	ūtor
ōra maritima	licet	altitūdō	nēmō
nāvis	rēs novae	adjiciō	cāritās
nāvigō	condiciō	accēdō	tālis
cōnsuēvī	ōdī	saeviō	tantus
ūsus	distribuō	vadum	sīc
initium	fīō	cōnsistō	ita
īdem	imperō (w. ut)	frūstrā	tam
permaneō	mandō (w. ut)	genus	adeō (adv.)
sententia	efficiō	ōrnātus	annus
aedificō	persuādeō	adversus (adj.)	certāmen
cōnfīdō	ostendō	vel (conj.)	paulō
adjungō	officium	singulī	lateō
arcessō	manus	cōnstat	unde
difficultās	celeritās	pugna	propinquus (adj.)

Vocabulary Chart No. 15

(Lessons 25-32, SECOND YEAR LATIN)

mare	nōtus	ob	prōdūcō
subitō	magnitūdō	dēsiliō	rūrsus
opportūnus	multitūdō	studium	clam
sōl	praemittō	decimus	discēdō
occāsus	imperātum	aquila	līberō
sōlis occāsus	domum	ūniversī	aedificium
aetās	ūnā	adorior	incolumis
āmittō	nactus	subsidium	neglegō
tollō	lītus	simul atque	avē
paucī	minimē	cursus	miserēre
dēsum	ancora	dēferō	nōlī (nōlīte)
aestās	at	accidit	quia
etsī	subsequor	trānsportō	quod (conj.)
īnsula	perspiciō	reficiō	quoniam
incognitus	morior	colloquor	cum (conj.)